The Signal Beneath the Noise

Discovering Your Inner Direction in a Distracted World

Deepanshu Suman

First Edition

2026

Copyright

The Signal Beneath the Noise

First Edition — 2026

ISBN: 978-93-5773-418-9

Author: Deepanshu Suman

Cover design and interior layout by the author.

Preface

Many people today live successful lives that quietly feel wrong.

From the outside everything appears stable work, responsibilities, progress. Yet internally there is a subtle sense that something about life does not fully fit.

This feeling is rarely dramatic. But it is persistent.

Information moves faster than reflection. Expectations arrive from every direction. Opinions, comparisons, advice, and narratives constantly compete for attention.

In such an environment, many people experience a quiet but persistent feeling: something in life feels slightly misaligned.

Nothing appears dramatically wrong.

They may be successful. They may have opportunities. They may even appear confident from the outside.

Yet internally, a question remains:

Why do I still feel lost?

For many people, this question creates a troubling assumption that something inside them must be missing.

But this book begins from a different premise.

People are not empty.

Most individuals already contain signals about who they are and what direction their lives might take. What prevents those signals from becoming clear is not a lack of purpose, but an excess of noise.

External expectations, constant comparison, cultural scripts, and digital distraction often drown out the internal patterns that quietly guide identity.

The Promise of This Book

This book is designed to help readers:

- Understand why it is possible to feel lost even in a world full of opportunity.
- Recognize the internal signals that reveal direction.
- Separate their authentic voice from the noise of social expectations.
- Discover patterns of attention, energy, and curiosity that reveal identity.
- Begin shaping a life that aligns with those patterns.

The goal is not to give you a predefined purpose.

The goal is to help you hear the signal that already exists.

Who This Book Is For

This book is written for readers who feel thoughtful but uncertain about their direction. In particular, it may resonate with:

- Adults between 18 and 40 navigating identity and career decisions.
- People in periods of transition who are questioning the path they are on.
- High-functioning individuals who appear successful but feel internally dissatisfied.
- Readers who seek depth and reflection rather than motivational slogans.

The Journey Through This Book

The chapters follow a psychological progression that mirrors how clarity develops.

1. **Recognition** — Realizing you are not alone in feeling uncertain.
2. **Understanding** — Learning why modern environments often create confusion.
3. **Separation** — Identifying which ambitions and expectations are not truly yours.

4. **Discovery** — Learning to observe the internal signals that reveal direction.
5. **Alignment** — Using those signals to design a life that fits who you are.

How the Book Is Structured

To guide this process, the book is organized into five parts and twenty chapters.

Each chapter contains four elements:

- Clear explanations of key ideas.
- Real-world examples that illustrate those ideas.
- Reflection prompts that help readers apply the ideas to their own lives.
- Transition insights that connect each chapter to the next stage of the journey.

The purpose of this book is not to tell you who you should become.

Instead, it invites you to notice something that has always been present:

your signal beneath the noise.

And once you begin to hear that signal, the question of direction stops feeling mysterious.

— *Deepanshu Suman*
2026

Part I

THE CONDITION OF DISCONNECTION

Chapter 1

The Quiet Sense That Something Is Off

There are moments in life when nothing appears dramatically wrong, yet something inside feels unsettled.

You wake up, move through your day, complete your responsibilities, and interact with the world in ways that seem normal perhaps even successful. From the outside, your life might appear stable or enviable.

Yet internally, a quieter experience sometimes emerges.

In small pauses during a commute, a quiet evening, or a moment of reflection you may notice a faint but persistent feeling that something about your life does not fully fit.

It is rarely a crisis. More often, it is subtle.

A low hum of dissatisfaction. A quiet question that briefly surfaces before being pushed aside.

Many people live with this feeling for years without fully naming it. They continue moving forward, meeting expectations and fulfilling responsibilities, while a quiet uncertainty remains beneath the surface.

Before any meaningful change can begin, this feeling must first be recognized.

This chapter explores that subtle sense of misalignment the quiet awareness that the life you are living may not fully reflect who you are.

1.1 Everyday Dissatisfaction

Most dissatisfaction in life does not arrive dramatically.

It does not begin with a crisis, a sudden loss, or a visible failure. In fact, it often appears when life seems to be working reasonably well. Responsibilities are being met. The future appears stable. From the outside, nothing seems obviously wrong.

Yet beneath this surface stability, a quieter feeling sometimes emerges.

It is difficult to name because it rarely takes the form of clear unhappiness. Instead, it appears as a subtle unease — a low, persistent sense that something about the way life is unfolding does not fully resonate.

Many people describe it as a vague restlessness.

Life continues to move forward, but something feels slightly out of tune. Days pass productively, but they blur together without leaving much emotional imprint. Achievements arrive, yet the satisfaction they produce fades quickly.

Because this dissatisfaction is subtle, it is easy to ignore.

People often rationalize it away. They tell themselves they should simply be grateful. After all, their circumstances might be far better than those of many others. The feeling may be dismissed as impatience, fatigue, or temporary stress.

Sometimes the explanation becomes a promise: things will feel different later.

Perhaps the next promotion will change it. Perhaps moving to a new city will change it. Perhaps the next stage of life will change it.

But often the feeling quietly returns.

Part of the reason this happens is that modern culture rarely encourages reflection on such feelings. Instead, it encourages momentum.

When uncertainty appears, the usual advice is to stay productive. Work harder. Set new goals. Keep moving forward.

Busyness becomes the solution to discomfort.

And in many ways, it works — at least temporarily. A full schedule leaves little space for uncomfortable questions. Activity fills the silence where reflection might otherwise occur.

But quiet dissatisfaction tends to reveal itself in the small gaps between activities.

It may appear during a commute when the mind begins to wander. It may surface late at night when distractions fade and the day finally slows down. It may emerge while listening to someone speak with genuine enthusiasm about something they care deeply about.

In those moments, you might notice a brief thought:

Why does my life not feel like that?

The feeling is rarely dramatic enough to demand immediate change. Most people simply continue with their routines, assuming that the sensation will eventually disappear.

Yet the fact that it continues to return suggests something else.

Quiet dissatisfaction is not always a sign that something is wrong.

Consider someone who has built a stable career in their late twenties.

From the outside their life appears successful. They have a respected job, steady income, and clear responsibilities. Yet during quiet moments perhaps while commuting home they sometimes notice a small question appearing:

Is this really what I want to keep doing?

Nothing dramatic is wrong, yet the feeling continues to return.

1.2 Functioning vs Living

One reason the quiet dissatisfaction described in the previous section can be difficult to recognize is that modern life is very good at rewarding *functioning.*

Functioning means operating effectively within systems. It means meeting expectations, completing responsibilities, staying organized, and progressing through recognized milestones. In many ways, functioning is necessary. Workplaces depend on it. Institutions are built around it. Entire cultures measure stability and success through it.

A person who functions well appears reliable and competent. They wake up on time, manage tasks, maintain commitments, and move steadily forward. From the outside, their life appears structured and successful.

But functioning and living are not the same experience.

It is entirely possible to function extremely well while feeling internally disconnected.

Consider someone who has built a stable career. Their work is respected.

Their schedule is full. Their responsibilities are handled efficiently. They are productive, organized, and dependable.

Yet when asked how they actually feel about the life they are living, their answer may be uncertain.

They are performing well, but something about the experience of living their life feels distant.

This is not unusual. In fact, it is quite common.

Modern societies place enormous value on efficiency and achievement. From an early age, people are encouraged to measure their progress through visible markers: grades, promotions, income, titles, accomplishments. These metrics are clear and widely recognized. They allow others to quickly assess whether someone is succeeding.

But these measures do not necessarily capture whether a person feels internally connected to what they are doing.

A person may become highly competent at something that never truly resonated with them.

They may master a profession, develop skills, and build an impressive record of achievements while quietly wondering why the experience of doing that work feels emotionally neutral.

Competence and alignment are not the same thing.

Competence means you are capable of performing something well. Alignment means the activity resonates with your deeper interests, values, or energy.

When competence and alignment coincide, work often feels engaging and meaningful. Effort still exists, but it is accompanied by a sense that one's abilities are being directed toward something that matters.

When competence exists without alignment, life can begin to feel mechanical.

You complete tasks successfully, but the satisfaction fades quickly. You move from one goal to the next without feeling deeply connected to the process. Progress continues, but it does not necessarily feel meaningful.

Many people interpret this feeling as laziness or ingratitude. They assume they simply need more discipline or a better attitude.

Yet often the issue is not effort or motivation.

It is alignment.

Living, in contrast to functioning, involves more than performing well within systems. It involves a sense that your actions, interests, and attention are moving in directions that feel authentically yours.

Living does not require constant excitement or dramatic purpose. Ordinary responsibilities still exist. Work still requires discipline. Life still includes routine.

But beneath those routines there is a sense of coherence.

Your actions feel connected to something inside you rather than merely responding to expectations outside of you.

The difference between functioning and living can be subtle, but it is deeply important.

Functioning asks: *Are you performing the required tasks?*

Living asks: *Does this life feel like it belongs to you?*

As you reflect on your own experience, it may be worth asking a simple question:

Right now, does your life feel more like functioning or truly living?

1.3 The Suppressed Question

For many people, the quiet dissatisfaction described earlier eventually gathers into a single, unspoken question.

It is rarely expressed aloud. Often it appears only briefly before being pushed aside.

The question is simple:

Is this really my life?

Not in the dramatic sense of wanting to abandon everything, but in a quieter and more reflective way. It asks whether the path you are currently following truly belongs to you — or whether it emerged gradually through expectation, circumstance, and momentum.

This question tends to appear in particular moments.

Sometimes it arises late at night, when the day's distractions fade and the mind becomes still. The routines of work and responsibility temporarily loosen their grip, and thoughts that were previously buried begin to surface.

At other times it appears after a milestone. A long-pursued goal is achieved — a promotion, a degree, a move to a new city. For a brief moment there is satisfaction, even relief. But once the excitement fades, an unexpected quiet may follow.

You might think: *Now what?*

Or more quietly: *Was this what I actually wanted?*

Transitions often bring the question into view as well. When life changes — finishing school, changing jobs, ending a relationship, moving somewhere new — the familiar structure that once guided daily life loosens. In that space of uncertainty, the deeper question sometimes rises to the surface.

Despite its importance, many people avoid engaging with it.

Part of the reason is practical. Life contains responsibilities, commitments, and expectations. Questioning one's path can feel destabilizing. It raises possibilities that may not have immediate answers.

Another reason is cultural.

Modern societies tend to reward certainty and forward momentum. Once someone has chosen a path — a career, a lifestyle, a set of goals — there is often subtle pressure to remain consistent. Doubt can be interpreted as weakness, indecision, or ingratitude.

People are encouraged to keep moving.

Work harder. Plan further ahead. Stay focused.

Reflection, especially reflection that questions the direction of one's life, can feel like an interruption to progress.

And so the question is often postponed.

People reassure themselves that they will think about it later — after the next promotion, after the next major project, after life becomes more stable. But "later" has a way of continuously moving forward.

Yet the question does not disappear.

Instead, it remains quietly present beneath daily activity, waiting for moments when the mind becomes still enough to hear it again.

This question is not a sign that something is wrong with you.

It may, in fact, be a sign that something within you is becoming more attentive.

To ask whether your life truly belongs to you is not an act of rebellion or dissatisfaction. It is an act of awareness.

And awareness is often the first step toward genuine self-understanding.

The chapters that follow will explore how identity, attention, and personal direction gradually become visible when we begin listening more carefully to our internal signals and learning to separate them from the noise surrounding us.

Chapter 2

Too Many Possible Lives

For most of human history, the shape of a life was largely predetermined.

People were born into communities where expectations were relatively clear. Work often followed family traditions. Social roles were defined early, and the path from youth to adulthood unfolded through familiar stages that most people recognized and shared.

This structure had many limitations. It restricted mobility, creativity, and personal choice. Yet it also provided something that modern life often struggles to offer:

orientation.

People generally knew what direction their lives were expected to take.

Today, the situation is very different.

Modern society offers an extraordinary range of possibilities. Careers that did not exist a generation ago are now common. People can change professions several times across their lives. Entirely new lifestyles and identities are visible and accessible through technology and global communication.

The number of possible ways to live has expanded dramatically.

In many ways, this expansion represents progress. Individuals now have far greater freedom to explore their interests, talents, and ambitions than at any previous time in history.

Yet this freedom carries an unexpected consequence.

When nearly every path appears possible, choosing a direction can become surprisingly difficult. The abundance of opportunity that once seemed liberating can gradually begin to feel overwhelming.

Instead of asking simply,

What should I do?

people often find themselves facing a more complicated question:

With so many possible lives available, how do I know which one is truly mine?

2.1 Explosion of Options

For much of human history, the range of possible lives was relatively narrow.

A person's work was often determined by geography, family tradition, or the needs of the local community. If your parents were farmers, artisans, or merchants, there was a strong chance that your own path would resemble theirs. Social roles were clear, and although these expectations could be limiting, they also reduced the burden of constant decision-making.

People did not spend years wondering what they should become.

The question was largely answered for them.

This did not mean life was easier or more fulfilling. Many individuals had little control over the direction their lives took. But the structure of society provided something modern life often lacks: a clear sense of orientation.

The path ahead was visible, even if it was narrow.

Today, that narrow path has widened into a vast landscape of possibilities.

Modern societies offer more career paths, lifestyles, and identities than at any other time in history. A person can become a software engineer, a designer, a teacher, a researcher, an entrepreneur, a content creator, a consultant, or pursue countless other professions that did not exist even a few decades ago.

Technology has accelerated this expansion. Through the internet, people are constantly exposed to new ways of living. One person builds a remote career while traveling across countries. Another creates a small business from their laptop. Someone else dedicates themselves to creative work, activism, or scientific research.

These possibilities can be inspiring.

They show us that life does not have to follow a single script.

But they also introduce a new and unfamiliar pressure.

When the number of available paths multiplies, each decision begins to feel heavier. Choosing one direction means not choosing many others. The more possibilities we see, the more aware we become of what we might be leaving behind.

A person deciding what career to pursue may not be choosing between two or three options. They may be comparing dozens of possibilities, each with its own promise and uncertainty.

Should you pursue financial stability or creative freedom?

Should you follow a profession you are skilled at, or explore something that feels more meaningful but uncertain?

Should you prioritize security, adventure, impact, independence, or recognition?

These questions do not have simple answers.

As a result, many people begin to feel responsible for designing their entire life from scratch.

In previous generations, life paths were often inherited. Today, they must often be invented.

This can feel empowering, but it can also feel overwhelming.

With so many visible possibilities, the responsibility for choosing the right one seems to fall entirely on the individual. If life turns out differently than expected, it can feel like a personal failure of judgment.

The abundance of choice that once appeared liberating slowly becomes something else.

Instead of providing clarity, it creates comparison. Instead of producing confidence, it creates hesitation.

And in the presence of too many possible lives, people often begin to experience an unexpected emotion:

anxiety.

2.2 Fear of Choosing Wrong

When the number of possible lives expands, decision-making begins to feel heavier.

Choosing a direction no longer feels like selecting one reasonable option. Instead, it can feel like determining the entire shape of the future.

Many people begin to experience a quiet but persistent fear:

What if I choose the wrong path?

This fear rarely appears in dramatic form. More often it emerges through subtle pressures that accumulate over time.

One of the strongest sources of pressure is the idea of a *timeline.*

Modern culture frequently presents life as a sequence of milestones that should occur at the correct moment. By a certain age, one should have chosen a career, built stability, achieved financial progress, and begun shaping the long-term structure of adult life.

These timelines are rarely stated directly, yet they appear constantly in conversations, media, and social comparison.

Someone notices that a friend has already established a successful career. Another person sees peers launching businesses, completing advanced degrees, or reaching visible markers of success. Gradually, an internal clock begins to form.

Am I falling behind? Should I already know what I am doing? Have I missed the right moment to choose?

This timeline pressure makes ordinary decisions feel urgent and irreversible.

Perfectionism intensifies this pressure.

If there are many possible paths, it becomes tempting to believe that one of them must be *the best.* Somewhere among the available options there must be a path that perfectly matches one's talents, interests, and future potential.

The challenge, of course, is identifying it.

People begin comparing choices endlessly. They research careers, analyze outcomes, and imagine long-term consequences. They ask themselves which option will produce the most success, the most stability, or the most meaning.

Instead of clarifying direction, this process often creates greater uncertainty.

Every path contains unknowns. Every decision involves trade-offs. Yet perfectionism encourages the belief that a completely optimal choice must exist if one thinks carefully enough.

Another source of anxiety emerges from the fear of wasted time.

Many people worry that choosing incorrectly will cost them years of effort that cannot be recovered. If they invest time in one field and later realize it is not right for them, they may feel that they have fallen behind those who chose correctly from the beginning.

This belief assumes that time spent on the "wrong" path is entirely lost.

But life rarely unfolds with that level of precision.

Skills accumulate in unexpected ways. Experiences that once seemed unrelated later become valuable. Relationships, knowledge, and personal insight often emerge from paths that initially appeared uncertain.

Yet when the fear of wasted time becomes dominant, people may hesitate to act at all.

They remain in a state of extended deliberation, hoping to discover the perfect decision before committing to any direction. Months pass, sometimes years, while the mind searches for certainty that never fully arrives.

The deeper assumption behind this fear is the belief that life contains a single correct path.

If that path can be identified early, everything will align. If it is missed, life will permanently drift away from its proper course.

But human lives rarely operate with that level of precision.

Most meaningful directions emerge gradually through exploration, adjustment, and unexpected discovery. People rarely identify their life's direction through a single decisive moment. Instead, they move through a series of choices that shape and reshape the path over time.

Seen this way, the question changes.

Instead of asking, *What is the one correct path I must choose right now?*

A different question becomes possible:

What is the next step that feels worth exploring?

Life may not unfold through one irreversible decision, but through a sequence of evolving choices that gradually reveal direction.

2.3 Freedom Without Orientation

For much of human history, the structure of adulthood was relatively clear.

While individuals certainly faced hardship and limitation, the general shape of life followed recognizable patterns. Work, family, and social responsibility unfolded according to expectations shared by the surrounding community. A person moved from youth into adulthood through stages that others had already experienced and understood.

These expectations did not eliminate uncertainty, but they provided orientation.

People knew, more or less, what came next.

Someone finished their education and entered a profession that often resembled the work of previous generations. Marriage and family tended to occur within predictable social timelines. Communities reinforced shared ideas about success, responsibility, and belonging.

Even when individuals questioned these expectations, they still understood the structure they were responding to.

In many parts of the modern world, those shared scripts have weakened.

Careers are less predictable. A single profession may evolve rapidly or disappear within a decade. People frequently change fields, retrain, or build entirely new forms of work. At the same time, family structures, relationships, and definitions of adulthood have become more diverse and less standardized.

These changes have expanded freedom in important ways.

Individuals can pursue education later in life. They can build unconventional careers. They can relocate, redefine relationships, and experiment with different lifestyles.

But the disappearance of clear scripts has also created a new challenge.

Without external guidance, people must increasingly design their lives themselves.

What once followed established patterns now requires personal decisions.

When should I choose a career? What kind of work should I pursue? Where should I live? What kind of relationships do I want to build? What does a meaningful life look like for me?

Each of these questions was once partially answered by culture, tradition, or community. Today they often fall entirely on the individual.

For some people, this autonomy feels exciting.

For others, it can feel disorienting.

Without shared expectations, there are fewer markers indicating whether one is moving in the right direction. People begin comparing themselves to a wide range of possibilities rather than a single cultural path. One friend may prioritize financial success, another creative expression, another stability and family life.

All of these paths appear legitimate.

But when every direction seems possible, it becomes difficult to know which one to trust.

In response, many people begin searching for external sources of certainty. They look to trends, public success stories, online advice, or cultural narratives about productivity and achievement. They try to identify what others consider the most impressive or meaningful way to live.

Yet these signals often conflict with one another.

One message encourages risk and entrepreneurship. Another promotes stability and long-term security. Some celebrate constant reinvention, while others emphasize commitment and discipline.

In the absence of shared scripts, the modern individual must navigate a landscape filled with competing signals.

Freedom, it turns out, is not always experienced as clarity.

Sometimes it feels like standing at a crossroads where every road appears open, yet none are clearly marked.

In such a world, direction cannot rely entirely on external guidance.

When cultural scripts become less reliable, something else must take their place.

Instead of looking outward for a predefined path, individuals may need to develop something more subtle but ultimately more dependable:

an internal compass capable of recognizing their own signal beneath the noise.

Chapter 3

Identity as Performance

There is a subtle shift that often occurs as people grow up.

In early life, identity tends to feel spontaneous. Children move naturally toward what captures their curiosity. They ask questions without hesitation, pursue interests without worrying about whether those interests appear impressive, and express emotions without carefully calculating how they will be perceived by others.

Their actions are guided mostly by curiosity rather than expectation.

But gradually, another force begins to shape behavior.

Expectation.

Family expectations. Educational expectations. Cultural expectations.

Over time, individuals begin to learn not only how to act, but how they are *supposed* to act.

The change is rarely dramatic. It happens slowly, almost invisibly, through everyday interactions and subtle forms of feedback. Certain behaviors are praised. Others are discouraged. Some paths are celebrated, while others are treated with uncertainty or concern.

Little by little, people adjust.

What begins as a natural process of social learning can eventually lead to something more profound. Identity, which once emerged from curiosity and internal experience, gradually becomes shaped by how one is expected to appear.

The difference may seem small at first.

Yet over time, this quiet adjustment can produce a significant transformation: identity begins to shift from something lived internally to something performed externally.

3.1 Roles Learned Early

Long before people consciously choose their direction in life, they begin learning how to occupy roles.

These roles are not usually assigned in formal ways. Instead, they emerge quietly through everyday interactions within the environments where early life unfolds: family, school, and the broader culture surrounding them.

Children are remarkably attentive observers. Even at a young age, they begin to notice patterns in how the world responds to them. Certain behaviors receive praise, encouragement, or attention. Others are ignored, corrected, or discouraged.

A child who finishes their homework carefully may hear that they are "responsible." Another who performs well in school may be described as "the smart one." A child who helps resolve conflicts among siblings may become known as "the peacemaker."

These labels often begin as simple observations. Yet repeated over time, they gradually shape how a person sees themselves.

Within families, these patterns can become particularly strong. Every household develops its own quiet distribution of roles. One child becomes the dependable one who can be trusted with responsibilities. Another becomes the adventurous one who challenges rules. Another may take on the role of the achiever, seeking approval through performance.

These identities are rarely chosen deliberately. Instead, they develop through subtle feedback. Children learn which behaviors bring recognition and which ones create tension. Over time, they begin adjusting their behavior accordingly.

Schools reinforce this process in different ways.

Educational institutions tend to reward behaviors that can be measured and evaluated. Attention, discipline, and academic performance are often emphasized because they can be observed and compared. Students quickly learn that certain qualities lead to recognition: high grades, leadership roles, participation in structured activities.

Those who perform well within these systems may begin to identify strongly with those achievements. They may come to see themselves as successful students, high performers, or reliable contributors.

Again, this process is not necessarily harmful. Learning responsibility, discipline, and cooperation can be valuable parts of development.

But there is an important psychological shift that can occur along the way.

When recognition becomes tied to specific behaviors, people may begin to orient their identity around those behaviors. The responsible one continues to take on responsibilities. The achiever continues to pursue measurable success. The dependable one becomes the person others rely on.

Over time, these roles can feel so familiar that they appear indistinguishable from identity itself.

Yet roles are only partial descriptions of who someone is.

A person who was praised for being dependable may also possess creativity that was never explored. Someone known as the achiever may quietly wonder about interests that do not produce immediate recognition. The roles that brought approval early in life may not fully capture the range of a person's curiosity, values, or inner motivations.

Roles can provide stability and structure. They help people function within families, schools, and communities.

But they do not necessarily reveal the deeper patterns of identity that emerge from within.

Understanding the roles we learned early in life is often the first step in recognizing that while those roles may have been useful, they may not fully represent who we truly are.

3.2 Approval as Compass

As people grow older and begin navigating larger social environments, another influence quietly begins shaping decisions: approval.

Approval is a powerful social force. Humans are deeply responsive to the reactions of others. A smile, a compliment, or a word of encouragement can feel energizing. Criticism, indifference, or disapproval can feel equally powerful in the opposite direction.

From an early age, people learn to notice these signals.

A student who receives praise for academic success may feel encouraged to continue pursuing that path. Someone who is recognized for leadership in group settings may begin to identify with being the person who organizes and directs others. Over time, these reactions begin to form patterns.

Certain behaviors produce positive responses. Others do not.

Gradually, people learn to orient themselves toward what receives recognition.

This process is not necessarily conscious. It happens slowly through repeated interactions. Praise from teachers, admiration from peers, encouragement from family members, and the visible status attached to certain careers or achievements all contribute to shaping the direction a person chooses.

Reputation becomes part of the equation.

Once people are known for something, they often feel pressure to maintain that image. The dependable employee continues taking on responsibility. The high-performing student continues striving for measurable success. The ambitious professional continues pursuing promotions and recognition.

These paths often make sense externally.

They are visible, respected, and socially validated. Success along these lines can bring opportunities, financial stability, and a sense of accomplishment.

Yet approval can also become something quieter and more influential.

It can become a compass.

When approval functions as a compass, decisions begin to revolve around how they will be perceived. A person may choose a career not only because it interests them, but because it signals intelligence, competence, or prestige. They may pursue goals that appear impressive even if those goals do not fully resonate with their deeper interests.

Sometimes this influence appears in subtle ways.

Someone might hesitate to explore a creative interest because it seems less practical than their current profession. Another person may continue pursuing a path they no longer enjoy simply because it would be difficult to explain a change to others.

The reactions of colleagues, friends, and family members become part of the internal calculation.

What will people think if I choose this direction? Will this decision make sense to others? Will it strengthen or weaken my reputation?

When these questions begin guiding decisions, approval gradually becomes an invisible form of navigation.

From the outside, the resulting path can look successful and coherent. The person appears disciplined, ambitious, and accomplished. Their identity aligns neatly with the expectations of the environments they inhabit.

But beneath that coherence, another question may quietly begin to form.

Is the direction being followed truly aligned with one's deeper interests and values or simply consistent with what others admire?

Approval can be a useful signal within social systems. It can highlight competence, reinforce effort, and encourage collaboration.

But when approval becomes the primary compass for decision-making, people gradually lose contact with signals that originate from within their own experience.

Yet it raises an important question.

Is approval always the same thing as alignment?

3.3 Losing Internal Reference

When identity becomes increasingly shaped by reputation and performance, something subtle can begin to fade.

At first, the change is almost invisible. A person adjusts their behavior to meet expectations, responds to recognition, and gradually builds a life that appears coherent and successful from the outside. They learn how to present themselves effectively, how to achieve results that others respect, and how to maintain a reputation that aligns with social standards.

From the outside, everything may appear to be working.

Yet the internal experience of living that life can slowly become more difficult to interpret.

This is the difference between external image and internal experience.

External image concerns how a life appears to others. It is built from visible markers: accomplishments, titles, achievements, reputation. These signals are easy for the world to recognize and measure.

Internal experience is quieter. It concerns how a life actually feels from within — the sense of engagement, curiosity, energy, or meaning that accompanies daily activity.

When people orient themselves primarily around external image, they may become very skilled at managing perception. They know how to present competence, how to navigate institutions, and how to pursue goals that earn recognition.

But in the process, they may begin to lose touch with a more subtle reference point.

Their own preferences.

Consider how easy it is for daily life to become structured around expectations. Work must be done efficiently. Professional goals must be pursued. Responsibilities must be fulfilled. Over time, routines become organized around what is required or rewarded rather than what feels internally meaningful.

A person may become so accustomed to performing certain roles that they rarely pause to ask whether those roles still reflect who they are.

Do I actually enjoy this work, or have I simply become good at it?

Do these goals still feel meaningful, or are they goals I learned to pursue years ago?

When life is lived primarily through performance, these questions may feel unfamiliar or even uncomfortable.

Another challenge emerges from the constant presence of external voices. Advice, expectations, cultural narratives about success, and social comparison all create a steady stream of signals about how a life should look.

Within that noise, one's internal voice can become difficult to hear.

The preferences that once appeared naturally — curiosity about certain subjects, excitement about certain activities, resistance toward others — may become faint beneath layers of expectation.

Sometimes people notice this disconnection only after significant time has passed.

A person may reach a milestone they worked toward for years and realize the satisfaction they expected does not arrive. Another may suddenly feel exhausted by a career that once seemed promising. Others may notice a vague sense that their life has been carefully constructed but not deeply inhabited.

In those moments, a quiet realization can emerge.

It is possible to build a life that looks right from the outside while feeling uncertain from within.

This realization can be unsettling, but it also marks an important turning point.

It suggests that beneath the roles, expectations, and performances of daily life, there remains another source of guidance — one that has simply grown quieter over time.

Rediscovering that internal reference point requires attention.

It means learning to notice the quiet signals that appear through curiosity, energy, and emotional response.

Those signals may have become faint beneath expectations, but they have not disappeared.

They are simply waiting to be heard again.

Chapter 4

The Comparison Machine

Human beings have always compared themselves to others.

In small communities, comparison served a practical function. People observed how others worked, solved problems, and navigated everyday challenges. These comparisons helped individuals learn, cooperate, and adapt within their environment.

But the scale of comparison has changed dramatically.

For most of history, people compared themselves to a relatively small circle: family members, neighbors, colleagues, and members of their local community. The reference points were limited, and most individuals lived under similar conditions, which made comparisons more grounded and easier to interpret.

Today the situation is very different.

Through phones, laptops, and constant connectivity, people are exposed to hundreds sometimes thousands of lives every day. Careers, lifestyles, achievements, relationships, travel experiences, creative accomplishments, and financial success appear continuously in a stream of images, updates, and stories.

This exposure has created something new in human experience.

A comparison machine.

Without consciously intending it, many people spend hours observing fragments of other people's lives. Each fragment may seem insignificant on its own, but together they accumulate, quietly shaping how individuals perceive their own progress, identity, and direction.

Over time, comparison stops being something we occasionally do.

It becomes part of the environment itself something that constantly surrounds our perception and subtly influences how we understand our own lives.

4.1 Curated Lives Everywhere

Modern technology has made it possible to observe the lives of others in a way that would have been unimaginable only a generation ago.

A person can open their phone at any moment and encounter a stream of images and updates from people living in different cities, professions, and cultures. Friends share milestones, colleagues announce achievements, acquaintances document travel, creativity, relationships, and personal growth.

At first glance, this constant visibility appears to offer connection. It allows individuals to remain aware of one another's lives across distance and time.

But the version of life presented on these platforms is rarely complete.

Online spaces tend to highlight moments that feel worth sharing: success, happiness, celebration, and visible progress. Promotions are announced. Projects are launched. Travel photos capture the most beautiful moments of unfamiliar places. Important milestones engagements, graduations, new homes, new ventures appear as polished snapshots.

These moments are genuine. They represent real experiences in people's lives.

Yet they are also carefully selected.

What rarely appears in these streams are the quieter, more ambiguous parts of life: uncertainty about career direction, long periods of effort without visible results, moments of doubt, frustration, or confusion. The internal process that often accompanies growth trial, error, hesitation, reconsideration is largely invisible.

The result is not deception, but incompleteness.

Each person shares fragments of their life that represent peaks rather than the full landscape. When these fragments from many different lives appear together in a single feed, the mind begins to assemble an impression that does not quite reflect reality.

It begins to look as though everyone else is progressing smoothly.

One person appears confident in their career path. Another seems deeply fulfilled in creative work. Someone else appears to be traveling, exploring, or building something meaningful.

Because these images arrive continuously, they gradually shape perception.

Even when individuals understand intellectually that social media represents a curated version of reality, the emotional effect can still be powerful. Repeated exposure to these fragments quietly shifts the way people interpret their own experiences.

Moments of uncertainty begin to feel unusual rather than normal. Periods of confusion seem like personal failures rather than natural parts of development.

A person who once viewed their life as an unfolding process may begin to see it through a different lens:

Why does everyone else seem more certain than I am?

Why does their progress appear clearer?

Why does my life feel less defined?

The comparison may not be intentional, but it becomes difficult to avoid. Each curated image becomes a subtle reference point against which one's own life is measured.

Over time, this constant exposure to curated lives begins to influence something deeper.

It quietly reshapes the standards by which people evaluate themselves.

4.2 Collapse of Self-Trust

When comparison becomes constant, it does more than influence mood. It gradually changes how people evaluate their own lives.

Psychologist Leon Festinger described this tendency as *social comparison theory* the idea that people naturally evaluate their abilities and progress by comparing themselves with others.

In earlier sections we explored how social environments expose individuals to curated fragments of other people's success and certainty. Over time, repeated exposure to these fragments begins to shift attention away from one's own lived experience and toward external benchmarks.

Instead of asking, *What feels meaningful to me?*, people may begin asking a different question:

How does my life compare to everyone else's?

This shift can happen quietly.

A person who once felt curious about a new direction might suddenly hesitate after seeing someone else's faster progress. Someone exploring a career path may begin wondering whether they are already behind because others appear to have moved further ahead. Even personal milestones career advancement, relationships, financial stability start to feel like positions on a shared timeline.

4.3 Signal vs Noise

At this point it becomes helpful to introduce a distinction that will guide the rest of this book: the difference between *signal* and *noise*.

A signal is a piece of information that carries meaningful direction. In the context of a human life, signals often appear through subtle internal experiences. They emerge through curiosity about certain subjects, through a sense of energy when engaging with particular problems, through emotional responses that quietly reveal what matters to us.

Signals are rarely loud.

In many ways, a human life resembles a communication system.

Signals carry meaningful information about direction, while noise consists of the surrounding interference that distorts that message.

When noise becomes overwhelming, the signal does not disappear— it simply becomes harder to recognize.

They do not usually appear as dramatic revelations or sudden clarity. More often they arise as small but persistent patterns.

You may notice that certain questions repeatedly capture your attention. Certain activities leave you feeling energized rather than drained. Certain ideas provoke genuine interest, while others feel strangely empty even when they appear impressive.

These experiences are signals.

They indicate where your attention naturally moves when it is not being directed by expectation or pressure. They reveal the contours of your values, interests, and deeper motivations.

Noise, by contrast, consists of the many external influences competing for attention.

Noise includes cultural expectations about success, trends that define what appears desirable, comparisons with other people's achievements, and social pressure to follow particular paths. It includes advice from well-meaning friends, professional norms, and the constant stream of opinions circulating through media and technology.

None of these influences are inherently harmful. In fact, many forms of external input can be useful. Advice can offer perspective, and cultural norms can provide structure.

The problem emerges when noise becomes overwhelming.

Modern environments amplify external signals at an unprecedented scale. Every day individuals encounter countless messages about what they should pursue, what success should look like, and how quickly progress should occur. Social media continuously displays examples of other people's milestones and achievements. Professional environments reinforce expectations about productivity and status.

In such an environment, noise becomes constant.

When noise is constant, attention naturally shifts outward. Instead of noticing internal signals curiosity, energy, emotional resonance people begin orienting themselves toward what appears visible and validated.

The difficulty is not that internal signals disappear.

They are simply quieter.

Curiosity rarely competes successfully with public recognition. Genuine interest is easily overshadowed by trends or status. Emotional signals about what feels meaningful can be drowned out by the steady rhythm of expectations.

Over time, this imbalance can make it difficult to recognize one's own direction.

A person may feel pulled in many directions at once. External signals offer advice, comparison, and examples of success, yet none of these signals fully resolve the deeper question of what actually belongs to them.

Learning to distinguish signal from noise becomes essential.

This distinction does not require rejecting the world around us or ignoring every external influence. Rather, it requires developing the ability to notice which signals arise from within and which originate from outside expectations.

Only when this difference becomes clear can a person begin to trust their own direction again.

The next part of this book will explore how these internal signals appear, how they can be recognized in everyday experience, and how learning to listen to them can gradually restore a sense of clarity in a world filled with noise.

Reflection Questions

1. What patterns appear in my attention?
2. Which activities increase my energy?
3. When did I last feel deeply engaged?

Part II

WHAT INNER DIRECTION REALLY IS

Chapter 5

Inner Direction Is Alignment

When people begin searching for direction in life, they often imagine that the answer will arrive as a sudden realization.

Perhaps it will appear as a moment of clarity. Perhaps there is a hidden calling waiting to be discovered. Perhaps one day everything will suddenly make sense.

But in reality, direction rarely appears that way.

For most people, direction is not revealed through a dramatic insight or a single life-changing decision. Instead, it develops gradually through a quieter process: alignment.

Alignment occurs when different parts of a person's inner life begin to work together. The things that capture their attention, the activities that give them energy, the values they care about, and the ways they express themselves in the world start to move in the same direction.

When these elements align, life begins to feel coherent. Effort still exists, uncertainty still appears, but there is a growing sense that one's actions make sense from the inside.

This chapter explores that idea more closely.

Rather than searching for a mysterious purpose or waiting for a moment of revelation, we will look at how inner direction often emerges from observing the patterns already present in one's own life.

The Signal Framework

Throughout this book we have explored a central idea: direction in life rarely appears as a sudden revelation. Instead, it emerges through a sequence of internal signals that gradually become visible when we learn how to observe them.

These signals form a simple structure that can help explain how personal direction develops.

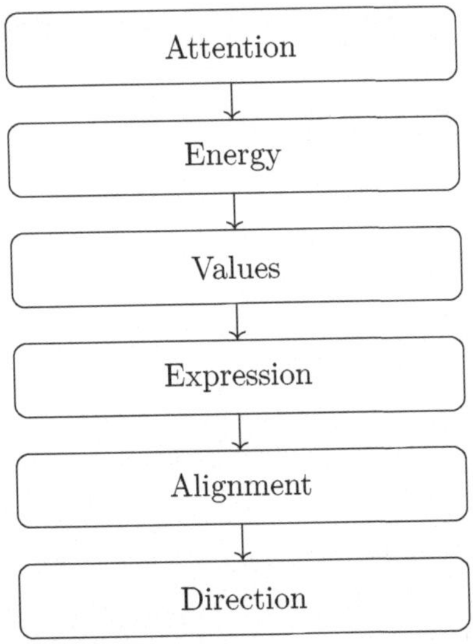

The framework begins with **attention**. What repeatedly captures your curiosity often reveals the subjects and problems your mind naturally gravitates toward.

Attention influences **energy**. Certain activities create vitality, focus, and sustained engagement, while others consistently drain motivation.

Over time, patterns in attention and energy reveal underlying **values**. These values shape what feels meaningful, important, or worth pursuing.

Values then influence **expression**. Expression refers to how a person naturally contributes, creates, communicates, or solves problems in the world.

When attention, energy, values, and expression reinforce one another, they create **alignment**. Life begins to feel more coherent because the different parts of a person's inner experience are moving in the same direction.

From alignment, **direction** gradually emerges.

Direction is therefore not something imposed from outside. It develops when internal signals become visible and begin guiding decisions.

This framework provides a practical way to understand the process explored throughout this book. Rather than searching for a predetermined purpose, individuals can observe these signals and allow direction to unfold naturally over time.

Consider someone whose attention repeatedly moves toward complex systems.

They notice patterns in technology, economics, or organizations. When working on these problems, their energy increases rather than declines.

Over time they realize that they value understanding how systems operate and improving them. Their expression may take the form of analysis, strategy, or design.

As these elements reinforce one another, alignment appears. From that alignment, direction gradually emerges.

5.1 Rejecting Mystical Explanations

When people begin searching for direction in life, they are often introduced to a powerful cultural narrative: the idea that everyone possesses a hidden purpose waiting to be discovered.

According to this narrative, somewhere beneath the confusion of everyday life there exists a single calling that perfectly defines who a person is meant to become. If one searches carefully enough or waits long enough there will eventually be a moment of revelation. Suddenly everything will become clear. The right path will appear, and the uncertainty that once dominated life will disappear.

This story is deeply appealing.

It suggests that confusion is temporary and that clarity exists somewhere beneath the surface. It implies that life contains a kind of hidden design waiting to be uncovered.

But there is a problem with this idea.

For most people, life does not unfold through dramatic revelations.

Instead, it unfolds through uncertainty, experimentation, gradual learning, and repeated adjustment. Direction emerges slowly, often in ways that are difficult to recognize in the moment.

When individuals expect purpose to appear as a sudden discovery, the absence of that moment can feel deeply discouraging.

A person may spend years waiting for a feeling of certainty that never arrives. They may believe that others have discovered something they have somehow missed. They may wonder whether they are lacking passion, discipline, or insight.

Questions begin to appear:

Why don't I know what I'm meant to do?

Why does everyone else seem more certain than I am?

Why hasn't my purpose revealed itself yet?

These questions can quietly create the impression that something is wrong with the person asking them.

But often nothing is wrong.

The difficulty lies in the expectation itself.

The idea of a single, predetermined calling assumes that identity is fixed and waiting to be uncovered. It treats direction as something that exists independently of experience as if the correct answer already exists and simply needs to be discovered.

Psychology suggests something very different.

Human identity is not static. It develops through interaction with experience, learning, and environment. Interests evolve. Skills develop over time. Values become clearer as individuals encounter situations that reveal what matters to them.

In other words, direction is rarely revealed.

It is constructed.

This construction does not occur randomly. It follows patterns that can be observed.

When people look carefully at their own lives, they often notice recurring tendencies. Certain subjects consistently capture their attention. Certain kinds of work feel naturally engaging. Some environments bring out their best thinking, while others drain their energy.

These patterns are signals.

They appear through curiosity, emotional responses, motivation, and the ways individuals naturally approach problems and ideas. They are not mystical messages or signs of destiny. They are psychological patterns that emerge from how a person's mind interacts with the world.

Understanding direction in this way changes the nature of the search.

Instead of waiting for a moment of revelation, the task becomes one of observation.

Where does your attention naturally go when you are free to choose?

What kinds of problems do you enjoy thinking about even when there is no immediate reward?

Which activities leave you energized rather than depleted?

These questions do not reveal a magical calling, but they do reveal patterns.

And patterns are far more reliable than sudden moments of inspiration.

When direction is understood through patterns rather than destiny, another important idea becomes visible: alignment.

Alignment occurs when the different elements of a person's internal life what they notice, what energizes them, what they value, and how they express themselves begin to move in the same direction.

When these elements are aligned, life begins to feel coherent. Work becomes more engaging. Decisions become easier. Effort produces a sense of meaning rather than exhaustion.

The goal, then, is not to discover a mystical purpose.

It is to understand how alignment emerges from the patterns already present within one's own experience.

The next section explores this idea more carefully by examining the four components that often shape inner direction: attention, energy, values, and expression.

5.2 Four Components of Alignment

If inner direction is not revealed through sudden insight or mystical discovery, how does it actually emerge?

One helpful way to understand it is through the idea of alignment.

Alignment occurs when several elements of a person's inner life begin to reinforce one another. Instead of pulling in different directions, these elements move together, creating a sense of coherence between how a person thinks, what they care about, and how they act in the world.

Although every individual is unique, four components often shape this alignment: attention, energy, values, and expression.

Understanding these components does not immediately solve the question of direction. But it provides a practical framework for observing the internal signals that gradually reveal it.

Attention

The first component is attention.

Attention reveals what naturally captures a person's curiosity. It shows where the mind tends to go when it is free to wander.

Some people repeatedly find themselves drawn to understanding how systems work technology, economics, organizations, or complex problems. Others are drawn toward human experience: relationships, emotions, communication, or cultural patterns. Some feel fascinated by creativity, design, storytelling, or artistic expression.

These patterns often appear early in life, but they are easy to overlook because they do not always correspond to formal achievements.

A person might spend hours reading about a particular topic simply because it is interesting. Another might frequently analyze how people behave in social situations. Someone else may feel naturally drawn toward building, designing, or improving things.

These recurring interests are signals of attention.

They indicate what the mind finds inherently engaging.

When direction aligns with attention, a person does not constantly struggle to stay interested. Curiosity itself helps sustain effort.

Energy

The second component is energy.

Energy refers to how different activities affect a person's sense of vitality.

Some activities create engagement and momentum. Even when they are difficult, they leave a person feeling mentally stimulated or satisfied. Other activities may appear reasonable or even prestigious, yet they leave a person feeling drained or detached.

For example, one person may spend hours solving technical problems and feel energized afterward. Another may feel deeply engaged while teaching, writing, designing, or organizing complex ideas. Yet those same activities might exhaust someone else.

Energy signals are often subtle, but they are consistent.

At the end of certain days, people feel mentally alive despite the effort they invested. At the end of other days, even relatively simple tasks can produce fatigue that feels deeper than physical tiredness.

These reactions provide important clues.

They reveal where a person's natural vitality tends to appear.

Values

The third component is values.

Values reflect the ideas and principles that feel genuinely important to a person.

Some individuals care deeply about understanding truth and knowledge. Others feel motivated by fairness, service, creativity, innovation, independence, or building things that last.

Values shape what kinds of goals feel meaningful.

For example, a person who values stability and responsibility may feel fulfilled building long-term systems that support others. Another who values exploration and creativity may feel more drawn toward experimentation and new ideas.

When values are ignored, even impressive achievements can feel strangely empty. A career may offer status or financial reward, yet still leave a person with the quiet sense that something essential is missing.

Alignment requires that one's activities resonate with what one genuinely considers important.

Expression

The fourth component is expression.

Expression refers to how a person naturally communicates, creates, or contributes to the world.

Two individuals may share the same interests and values yet express them in very different ways. One person may express ideas through writing. Another through teaching, building organizations, designing systems, creating art, or solving complex problems.

Expression is the outward form through which inner patterns become visible.

It reflects how a person tends to organize their thoughts and translate them into action.

When expression fits a person's natural tendencies, effort feels more fluid. Ideas move more easily from thought into action.

Alignment

Each of these components attention, energy, values, and expression offers a partial signal about direction.

Individually, they provide hints.

Together, they create alignment.

Alignment occurs when the things that capture a person's attention also generate energy, reflect their values, and find a natural form of expression in the world.

For example, someone whose attention is drawn toward complex systems, who feels energized by solving difficult problems, who values intellectual exploration, and who expresses ideas through research or analysis may gradually find themselves aligned with work that involves investigation, design, or strategic thinking.

Another person whose attention gravitates toward human experiences, who gains energy from communication, who values empathy and connection, and who expresses themselves through teaching or storytelling may find alignment in roles that involve guiding or helping others.

The specific outcomes vary widely. What matters is the coherence between these internal elements.

When alignment begins to appear, direction stops feeling mysterious. Decisions become easier to interpret. Activities that once seemed unrelated start forming recognizable patterns.

Instead of searching for a hidden purpose, people can begin observing how these components interact within their own experience.

Learning to notice attention, energy, values, and expression provides a practical way to recognize the signals already present beneath the noise.

5.3 Fit vs Achievement

Modern culture often treats achievement as evidence that a person has found the right path.

When someone becomes successful earning recognition, financial stability, or professional status it is easy to assume that their work must also feel meaningful to them. From the outside, success appears to confirm that a life is moving in the correct direction.

Yet the internal experience of success is often more complicated.

It is entirely possible for a person to become highly accomplished while quietly feeling disconnected from the life they have built. They may perform their work effectively, earn respect from others, and continue progressing along a visible career path, yet still feel a persistent sense that something is missing.

This situation is more common than it first appears.

Part of the reason lies in the difference between competence and alignment.

Competence refers to the ability to perform something well. A person can become competent in many areas through discipline, training, and repeated effort. Over time, they may develop strong skills, gain recognition, and produce impressive results.

Alignment, however, concerns something different. It refers to the degree to which a person's work reflects their internal patterns their attention, energy, values, and natural forms of expression.

A person may become competent at tasks that do not truly engage them.

Consider someone who excels in a profession because they are disciplined and intelligent. They learn the systems, master the expectations, and perform well within the environment. Promotions follow. Recognition grows.

Yet when they pause to reflect, they may notice that their work rarely produces genuine curiosity or excitement. It feels manageable, sometimes even rewarding, but not deeply engaging.

Their competence is real, but their alignment is weak.

External rewards can make this distinction difficult to notice.

Recognition, income, and status create powerful signals that reinforce the idea that one is on the correct path. Friends and colleagues may admire the achievements. Society may label the life as successful.

These signals can temporarily obscure internal dissatisfaction.

A person may assume that if they have reached visible milestones, fulfillment should eventually follow. If meaning has not appeared yet, perhaps it will arrive after the next promotion, the next project, or the next stage of achievement.

But over time, the quiet gap between external success and internal experience can become more noticeable.

The work continues to produce results, yet it does not produce the sense of coherence that often accompanies alignment. Effort remains constant, but the energy behind that effort gradually weakens.

This is why fit matters.

Fit refers to the relationship between a person's internal patterns and the environment in which they operate. When fit is strong, a person's attention, energy, values, and expression reinforce the work they are doing. Even when challenges arise, the activity still feels connected to something internally meaningful.

When fit is weak, the opposite occurs.

A person may still perform well, but the work requires continuous effort to maintain motivation. Over time, the absence of alignment can produce fatigue, confusion, or the subtle feeling that one is living a life that makes sense to others but not entirely to oneself.

None of this means that achievement is unimportant.

Accomplishment can provide stability, opportunity, and the ability to contribute meaningfully to the world. But achievement alone cannot determine whether a path truly fits the person walking it.

Only alignment can reveal that.

When a person's attention, energy, values, and expression move together, direction begins to feel clearer from the inside. Success may still follow, but it is no longer the primary signal guiding decisions.

Instead, the more reliable indicator becomes alignment itself.

Inner direction is not defined by how impressive a life appears from the outside, but by how coherently its parts fit together from within.

Chapter 6

Personal Patterns

When people search for direction, they often assume the answer lies somewhere ahead of them.

They imagine that clarity will arrive through a new opportunity, a decisive choice, or a sudden realization about what they should do with their life. The future becomes the place where direction is expected to appear.

But direction does not always emerge by looking forward.

Often it becomes visible by looking backward.

Human identity tends to leave traces. Over time, patterns appear in the things people repeatedly notice, the problems they enjoy thinking about, and the ways they respond to the world around them. These patterns are rarely dramatic, yet they are often remarkably consistent.

At first they are easy to overlook. Interests seem casual, habits appear ordinary, and preferences develop gradually through everyday experience.

Yet when viewed across years rather than moments, these small tendencies begin to form recognizable shapes.

The mind repeatedly returns to certain kinds of questions. Energy appears in particular kinds of activities. Certain ways of thinking or interacting feel natural, while others require constant effort.

These are personal patterns.

Rather than representing a predetermined destiny, they reflect the structure of a person's attention, motivations, and cognitive tendencies. They reveal how someone naturally engages with ideas, problems, and other people.

Learning to observe these patterns can reveal more about direction than waiting for a single moment of clarity.

Instead of searching for a dramatic revelation, a person can begin by noticing the signals already present within their own experience.

6.1 Recurring Interests

One of the most reliable clues about a person's inner direction appears in something surprisingly simple: what repeatedly captures their attention.

Across years sometimes even decades certain topics, questions, and activities continue to draw a person's curiosity. These interests may appear in different forms, yet they often revolve around similar themes.

Someone might repeatedly find themselves fascinated by how systems work. They enjoy understanding organizations, technologies, or complex structures. Another person may feel consistently drawn toward understanding people why individuals behave the way they do, how relationships function, or how communication shapes human experience.

Others may experience a recurring pull toward creativity: designing things, telling stories, building objects, or turning abstract ideas into tangible form.

These interests often appear quietly.

They show up in the books someone chooses to read, the conversations they enjoy most, the topics they research without being required to, or the problems their mind returns to when it has time to wander.

A person might notice that whenever they enter a bookstore, they gravitate toward the same section. Another may find themselves repeatedly watching documentaries about similar subjects. Someone else might spend hours exploring ideas online that have little connection to their formal responsibilities.

At first, these tendencies may seem insignificant.

People often assume that real direction must come from practical considerations such as career opportunities, financial stability, or social expectations. Curiosity, by contrast, can appear too casual to matter.

But curiosity is rarely random.

When the mind repeatedly returns to certain themes, it often reveals something about how a person naturally engages with the world. Curiosity tends to follow patterns that reflect deeper interests and motivations.

Yet many people learn to ignore these signals.

Sometimes recurring interests appear impractical. A fascination with storytelling might seem irrelevant to someone pursuing a technical profession. An interest in psychology might feel disconnected from a career in finance. Curiosity about design, education, or philosophy may appear unrelated to the demands of everyday work.

Because these interests do not always align with visible opportunities, people may treat them as hobbies or passing distractions rather than meaningful clues.

Over time, however, patterns of curiosity often reveal something more substantial.

A person who repeatedly explores how ideas are communicated may eventually discover that teaching, writing, or explaining complex topics feels natural. Someone who consistently analyzes systems may later find themselves drawn toward strategy, engineering, or problem-solving roles.

The specific interests may evolve, but the underlying themes often remain surprisingly stable.

Recurring fascination frequently signals alignment between how a person's mind works and the kinds of questions they feel compelled to explore.

This does not mean every interest should immediately become a career. But it does suggest that repeated curiosity deserves attention.

Instead of dismissing these patterns as trivial, it may be more useful to ask:

What topics have quietly followed me throughout my life?

Which questions have returned again and again, even when I tried to focus on something else?

The answers to those questions often reveal signals that have been present for years waiting to be noticed.

6.2 Behavioral Tendencies

In addition to recurring interests, another set of patterns often reveals itself through behavior.

People tend to approach the world in consistent ways. When faced with problems, decisions, or interactions with others, certain styles of thinking and responding appear again and again.

These patterns are rarely obvious in the moment. They simply feel natural to the person expressing them. But when observed across time and different situations, they begin to form recognizable tendencies.

Consider how different individuals approach a challenge.

One person might immediately begin analyzing the structure of the problem. They break it into parts, identify relationships between variables, and search for logical solutions. Another person might focus first on the people involved. They try to understand motivations, emotions, and how communication might resolve tension.

Both approaches can be effective, yet they reflect very different cognitive tendencies.

Similar differences appear in how people interact with others.

Some individuals naturally take initiative in group situations. When a discussion becomes uncertain, they begin organizing ideas, proposing plans, or coordinating action. Others prefer to observe first, absorbing information and considering possibilities before speaking.

Some communicate best through structured explanation, carefully organizing ideas into clear frameworks. Others communicate through conversation, exploring ideas dynamically as they interact with others.

Over time, these tendencies become part of how a person navigates the world.

They also influence which environments feel comfortable or productive.

A person who enjoys deep analytical thinking may thrive in environments that allow extended concentration and complex problem-solving. Someone whose strengths lie in communication and interpersonal awareness may feel energized in collaborative settings where interaction and discussion are central.

When environments match a person's natural tendencies, behavior flows easily. Effort still exists, but it feels sustainable. Work becomes an extension of how the person already thinks and acts.

When environments clash with these tendencies, the opposite often occurs. Tasks require constant adjustment, and even simple responsibilities can feel exhausting because they conflict with the person's natural style.

Importantly, these tendencies tend to remain surprisingly stable across different contexts.

A person who enjoys organizing ideas in school may later find themselves structuring projects at work. Someone who naturally mediates disagreements among friends may later gravitate toward roles involving negotiation or leadership. An individual who enjoys exploring complex systems may consistently seek environments where analysis and strategy are valued.

The specific settings may change, but the underlying patterns remain.

These behavioral tendencies offer important clues about identity. They reveal not just what people are interested in, but how they prefer to engage with challenges, relationships, and ideas.

Understanding these tendencies can therefore become a practical guide.

Rather than forcing oneself to fit environments that constantly demand unnatural behavior, a person can begin looking for contexts where their natural tendencies are not obstacles but strengths.

In those environments, the patterns that once felt ordinary begin to reveal their deeper significance.

6.3 Pattern Recognition Method

If identity reveals itself through patterns, the next question becomes practical: how can a person begin noticing those patterns clearly?

Most people move through life responding to immediate demands. Work requires attention, responsibilities accumulate, and decisions are made under pressure or necessity. In such conditions, it is easy to overlook the quieter signals that appear within everyday experience.

Pattern recognition requires a different posture.

A simple exercise can make these patterns easier to see.

Write down three moments from the past year when you felt deeply engaged in what you were doing. Then ask what those moments had in common.

Often the similarities reveal patterns that were previously invisible.

It asks a person to step slightly outside the flow of events and observe their own behavior over time.

Instead of asking abstract questions about purpose, the process begins with simple observation.

One starting point is to notice recurring interests across different stages of life.

Think about the topics or activities that have appeared repeatedly over the years. These interests may have taken different forms at different times. A childhood fascination with drawing might later appear as an interest in design or visual communication. An early curiosity about how machines work might evolve into an interest in engineering, systems, or technology.

The specific expression may change, but the underlying curiosity often remains consistent.

Another useful observation concerns moments of energy and engagement.

Certain situations create a sense of mental vitality. Time passes quickly, attention becomes focused, and effort feels meaningful rather than draining. These experiences do not necessarily involve ease or comfort sometimes they appear while solving difficult problems or working through complex ideas but they carry a sense of engagement that feels distinct from routine obligation.

Reflecting on such moments can reveal important signals.

When during the past year did you feel most mentally alive? What kinds of tasks absorbed your attention without requiring external pressure?

A third area involves observing recurring behaviors.

People often display consistent tendencies in how they approach work, relationships, and learning. Some individuals naturally explain ideas to others. Some instinctively organize complex information. Others connect people, generate creative possibilities, or refine existing systems.

These tendencies may appear across very different environments.

Someone who enjoyed organizing group projects in school might later coordinate teams at work. A person who often explained ideas to friends may later gravitate toward teaching, writing, or mentoring. The contexts change, but the behavior remains recognizable.

The final step is to connect these observations.

Instead of viewing each experience separately, begin looking for patterns that link them together. Recurring interests, moments of energy, and behavioral tendencies often point toward the same underlying themes.

For example, a person who repeatedly explores ideas, enjoys explaining concepts, and feels energized when teaching may discover that communication and knowledge-sharing form a central pattern in their identity.

Another person who frequently analyzes systems, enjoys solving complex problems, and organizes information instinctively may notice a pattern of analytical thinking that shapes many aspects of their life.

This process does not produce a single fixed answer about what someone must do.

Rather, it gradually reveals the structure of how a person naturally engages with the world.

When these patterns become visible, something important begins to change.

Decisions no longer depend entirely on external comparison or expectation. Instead, they can be guided by signals that emerge from within one's own experience.

Recognizing personal patterns does not eliminate uncertainty.

But it often restores something that modern environments frequently weaken: the ability to trust one's own internal signals again.

Reflection Questions

1. What patterns appear in my attention?
2. Which activities increase my energy?
3. When did I last feel deeply engaged?

Chapter 7

Energy as Compass

People often search for direction by thinking about goals, plans, and long-term ambitions.

They ask themselves what career they should pursue, what achievements they should aim for, or what kind of life they should build in the future. These questions are important, but they sometimes overlook a quieter source of information that appears within everyday experience.

Energy.

Across the course of ordinary days, people move through many different activities meetings, conversations, problem-solving, learning, planning, and creative work. Yet not all activities feel the same from the inside. Some leave a person feeling mentally alive and engaged. Others create a subtle resistance that makes even simple tasks feel heavier than they should.

Most people have noticed this difference.

Certain tasks absorb attention so completely that hours pass without being noticed. Others require constant effort just to remain focused. Some conversations feel stimulating and leave a person thinking about them long afterward. Others create an immediate desire to withdraw.

These variations are not random.

They are signals.

Energy patterns often reveal how well a person's activities align with their natural interests, thinking style, and values. When alignment is strong, effort can still be demanding, but it carries a sense of engagement that makes the work feel meaningful. When alignment is weak, even routine tasks can gradually become exhausting.

Learning to observe these patterns can provide something surprisingly useful: a practical compass for understanding personal direction.

7.1 Vitality Signals

If energy can function as a compass, one of the clearest signals it provides appears in moments of vitality.

Vitality does not necessarily mean excitement or enthusiasm in a dramatic sense. It is often quieter than that. It appears when attention settles naturally on an activity and remains there without constant effort. The mind becomes engaged, distractions fade, and the work itself begins to hold interest.

Many people have experienced this state at different points in their lives.

A person solving a complex problem may become so absorbed in the process that hours pass without being noticed. Someone writing, designing, or building something may suddenly look up and realize far more time has passed than expected. A conversation about a meaningful topic may extend far beyond its original purpose because both participants feel mentally stimulated.

In these moments, effort still exists. Concentration is required, and the activity may even be challenging. Yet the effort does not feel forced. Attention seems to organize itself around the task rather than being constantly pulled away from it.

Psychologists sometimes describe this experience as deep engagement or focused immersion. But even outside of such intense states, smaller signals of vitality appear in everyday life.

A person might notice that they feel unusually alert while discussing certain subjects. Another might feel energized after teaching someone a new concept. Someone else might find that organizing information, solving technical problems, or exploring ideas creates a quiet sense of satisfaction.

These reactions are easy to overlook because they often feel ordinary.

But their consistency matters.

When a person repeatedly experiences vitality around particular kinds of activities, it suggests a form of alignment between their attention, cognitive style, and underlying interests. The activity fits the way their mind naturally operates.

For example, someone whose attention is drawn toward understanding systems may feel energized when analyzing complex structures or solving strategic problems. Another person may experience vitality in situations involving communication, explanation, or helping others understand difficult ideas.

These signals do not always correspond to formal achievements or obvious talents. A person may feel deeply engaged in an activity long before they develop strong skill in it. What matters is not immediate competence but the presence of sustained attention and curiosity.

Over time, vitality signals tend to repeat.

Certain environments consistently produce engagement. Certain types of work repeatedly capture attention. Certain conversations, problems, or creative efforts leave a person mentally stimulated rather than depleted.

Noticing these patterns can provide valuable information.

Instead of asking only what you should pursue in the future, it can be useful to ask a simpler question:

When do I feel most mentally alive?

Pay attention to the situations where your focus deepens, where effort feels meaningful rather than forced, and where time seems to pass more quickly than expected.

These moments often reveal where alignment already exists.

7.2 Drain Signals

If vitality reveals where alignment may exist, exhaustion often reveals where it does not.

Every activity requires some degree of effort. Even work that feels meaningful can produce fatigue, especially after long periods of concentration or responsibility. Temporary tiredness is therefore not a reliable signal by itself.

But some forms of fatigue behave differently.

Certain tasks consistently feel heavier than they should. They require disproportionate effort to begin and even more effort to sustain. A person may notice that they procrastinate repeatedly, even when they understand the importance of the task. When the work is finally completed, the feeling is often not satisfaction but relief that it is finished.

These experiences are examples of drain signals.

Drain signals appear when an activity consistently produces mental resistance, boredom, or exhaustion that goes beyond normal effort. The task may still be manageable, and the person may even perform it well, yet the experience of doing it feels persistently draining.

For example, someone who naturally enjoys analytical thinking may feel exhausted by environments that require constant social negotiation and emotional management. Another person who thrives in collaborative settings may feel depleted when working alone for long stretches with minimal interaction.

The difference is not about ability.

In many cases, individuals can perform these tasks competently. With discipline and practice, most people can adapt to environments that do not naturally suit them. The problem arises when this adaptation becomes permanent.

Over time, sustained misalignment often produces chronic fatigue.

The person may begin each day with a sense of reluctance. Tasks that once felt neutral gradually become burdensome. Concentration becomes harder to maintain, and even after rest the same activities continue to feel draining.

It is important to distinguish these signals from ordinary tiredness.

Temporary fatigue usually has a clear cause: lack of sleep, intense effort, or a particularly stressful period. After recovery, energy returns and engagement becomes possible again.

Chronic misalignment behaves differently.

Even after adequate rest, the same activities continue to produce resistance. The environment itself seems to drain energy rather than restore it.

Despite these signals, many people learn to ignore them.

Obligation often plays a role. Responsibilities must be fulfilled, deadlines must be met, and practical considerations such as income or stability can make it difficult to reconsider one's environment. Social expectations also reinforce persistence. When others view a path as successful or respectable, questioning it can feel uncomfortable or even irresponsible.

As a result, people may continue investing energy in roles that consistently leave them depleted.

From the outside, everything appears functional. Work continues to be completed. Progress may still occur. Yet internally the cost grows heavier over time.

Drain signals are not always instructions to abandon a responsibility immediately. Many meaningful pursuits contain periods of difficulty that require perseverance.

But when the same forms of exhaustion appear repeatedly across months or years, they may be communicating something important.

They may be indicating areas where alignment is missing.

7.3 Burnout as Feedback

Burnout has become a familiar term in modern conversations about work and mental health. It is often described as a state of exhaustion in which motivation disappears, concentration weakens, and even routine responsibilities begin to feel overwhelming.

In many discussions, burnout is framed primarily as a problem of endurance. The explanation tends to focus on excessive workload, poor time management, or a lack of resilience. When someone feels burned out, the usual advice is to rest, improve productivity systems, or develop stronger coping strategies.

These responses can be helpful, but they sometimes overlook an important possibility.

Burnout may not simply be the result of working too hard. It may also be the result of working in ways that are deeply misaligned.

To understand this, it helps to consider how burnout usually develops.

Most people do not suddenly become exhausted overnight. Instead, the process tends to unfold gradually. A person may spend months or years performing work that requires continuous effort but produces little sense of engagement. Responsibilities accumulate, expectations increase, and the individual continues pushing forward out of discipline or obligation.

At first, the effort feels manageable. But over time, the internal cost begins to rise.

Energy declines. Tasks that once felt neutral begin to feel burdensome. The person may notice a growing sense of detachment from their work or environment. Eventually, even small responsibilities can feel overwhelming because the internal resources required to perform them have been steadily depleted.

When this happens, burnout is often interpreted as a personal failure.

A person may believe they lack discipline, motivation, or mental toughness.

They may compare themselves to others who appear capable of sustaining similar workloads and conclude that something must be wrong with them.

But another explanation is often more accurate.

Burnout frequently appears when effort is sustained in environments that do not match a person's natural patterns of attention, energy, and values. The individual may be competent enough to function within that environment, but the work itself requires constant psychological adjustment.

Imagine someone whose natural tendencies involve creativity, exploration, and generating new ideas working within a rigid system that prioritizes strict procedures and repetitive tasks. Or consider a person energized by collaboration placed in an isolated environment where interaction is minimal.

In both cases, the person may still perform effectively for some time.

But sustaining that performance requires continuous effort against their natural tendencies. Over long periods, that effort can gradually erode motivation and emotional energy.

Viewed from this perspective, burnout begins to look less like failure and more like feedback.

It signals that the current arrangement between a person and their environment may not be sustainable. Something about the structure of the work, the expectations placed upon the individual, or the direction being pursued is not aligned with the way that person naturally functions.

This does not mean that every experience of burnout requires an immediate or dramatic change. Sometimes adjustments to workload, boundaries, or rest can restore balance.

But burnout often invites a deeper question.

Instead of asking only how to recover enough energy to continue the same path, it may be worth asking what the exhaustion itself is trying to reveal.

What aspects of this environment consistently drain energy? Which responsibilities feel disconnected from personal interests or values? What kinds of activities still produce engagement, even in small amounts?

When burnout is understood as feedback rather than weakness, it can become a source of insight.

The exhaustion does not simply mark the end of endurance. It marks the point where the current direction may need to be reconsidered.

In this way, burnout can serve as one of the clearest signals that alignment between a person and their work or their broader life direction has begun to break down.

Chapter 8

Emotional Signals

In everyday conversation, emotions are often treated as distractions.

People talk about controlling their feelings, suppressing them, or preventing emotions from interfering with rational decisions. In professional environments especially, emotional responses are sometimes viewed as signs of weakness or a lack of discipline.

Yet emotions did not evolve to disrupt human thinking.

They evolved to inform it.

Every emotional reaction contains information about how a person is experiencing the world around them. Excitement, frustration, curiosity, anxiety, satisfaction, and disappointment are not random disturbances. They are signals that reveal how our experiences interact with our expectations, needs, and values.

Most of the time, these signals operate quietly in the background of awareness. People notice the feeling itself but rarely pause to consider what it might be indicating.

But if identity and direction emerge through patterns of internal signals, emotions are among the most immediate signals available. They appear quickly, often before conscious reasoning has had time to interpret a situation.

Learning to observe emotional responses more carefully can therefore reveal something important: how closely a person's life aligns with what truly matters to them.

8.1 Emotions as Data

If emotions are treated only as disturbances, an important source of information is lost.

In many environments people are encouraged to separate emotion from decision-making. Rational thought is often presented as clear and reliable, while feelings are viewed as unpredictable influences that must be controlled or suppressed.

But this distinction is misleading.

Emotions are not the opposite of reasoning. They are part of the system that helps human beings evaluate what is happening around them. When a situation occurs, the mind does not simply process facts. It also generates emotional responses that signal how that experience relates to our expectations, priorities, and values.

In this sense, emotions function as a kind of internal data.

Consider how quickly emotional reactions appear. A person might feel interest during a conversation, irritation during a meeting, anxiety before presenting an idea, or satisfaction after completing a meaningful task. These responses often arise before conscious analysis has had time to interpret the situation.

This speed exists for a reason.

Emotions evolved as a way for the mind to summarize complex information quickly. Instead of calculating every possible implication of an experience, the brain produces a signal that indicates how the experience relates to personal needs, goals, or concerns.

For example, curiosity often appears when something new aligns with a person's interests. The emotional pull toward learning more reflects a signal that the topic is mentally engaging. Frustration may appear when obstacles block progress toward something important. Satisfaction may arise when effort produces a result that matches one's expectations.

These reactions reveal more than momentary feelings.

They often reflect deeper priorities.

Imagine two people attending the same professional meeting. One person feels energized by the discussion of new ideas and future possibilities. The other feels bored and disengaged. The meeting itself is identical for both individuals, yet their emotional responses differ because their internal priorities differ.

One finds meaning in that environment. The other does not.

Emotions therefore provide clues about what matters to us.

They signal when an activity resonates with our interests or values, and they also signal when something feels misaligned with them.

Ignoring these signals can make self-understanding more difficult.

Many people learn to dismiss their emotional reactions in order to meet external expectations. A job may produce constant frustration, but the feeling is ignored because the position offers status or security. A creative interest may produce excitement, yet the person dismisses it as impractical.

Over time, this habit of ignoring emotional responses can obscure important information.

When signals are repeatedly dismissed, it becomes harder to recognize what genuinely engages or concerns us. Life decisions may then rely almost entirely on external criteria income, prestige, or comparison with others while the internal signals that once indicated alignment grow faint.

This does not mean that every emotion should be followed immediately.

Emotions can be influenced by temporary stress, misunderstanding, or incomplete information. They are signals, not instructions.

But signals still matter.

When emotional responses are observed carefully especially when they appear repeatedly across different situations they begin to reveal patterns about what a person values, fears, enjoys, or finds meaningful.

In this way, emotions can become something more than passing reactions.

They can become guides.

8.2 Hidden Clues

If emotions function as data, some of the most useful signals come from feelings that people often misunderstand.

Certain emotions carry information about hidden priorities, interests, or concerns that may not yet be fully conscious. When examined carefully, these reactions can reveal clues about what a person values or fears, even when those priorities have not been clearly articulated.

Take envy as an example.

Envy is usually treated as an emotion to suppress. It is associated with resentment or comparison, and many people feel uncomfortable acknowledging it. Yet envy often points toward something meaningful.

When someone feels envious of another person's achievements, the reaction may indicate more than simple comparison. It may reveal an unrecognized aspiration.

A person who feels envy toward someone building a creative career may discover that creativity matters to them more than they previously admitted. Another person who envies a colleague's independence may realize that autonomy is a deeper priority than they once believed.

In this sense, envy can function as a directional signal. It highlights something that appears valuable from the observer's perspective.

Curiosity offers another important clue.

Unlike envy, curiosity is usually experienced as a positive emotion. It appears when a subject captures attention and creates the desire to explore further. People often feel curious about topics that resonate with their natural interests or cognitive tendencies.

Someone might repeatedly find themselves drawn toward understanding technological systems, human psychology, economic patterns, or artistic expression. These interests may appear casually at first a book that captures attention, a conversation that becomes unexpectedly engaging, or a question that continues returning to the mind.

Over time, these moments of curiosity often form patterns.

The mind tends to explore certain kinds of questions more than others. When these patterns are observed across years rather than isolated moments, they can reveal enduring intellectual interests that shape a person's direction.

Anxiety provides another kind of signal, although it is often more difficult to interpret.

Many people experience anxiety when approaching situations that involve uncertainty or risk. Speaking in public, changing careers, pursuing creative work, or expressing unconventional ideas can all trigger anxious responses.

At first glance, anxiety appears purely negative. But in many cases it indicates that something feels significant.

A person may feel anxious about presenting an idea not because they are incapable of doing so, but because the idea matters to them. The emotional intensity reflects the perceived importance of the situation.

Of course, anxiety can also arise from perceived threats or unrealistic fears. Interpreting it requires careful attention. Yet even then, the emotion signals that something about the situation deserves examination.

When these emotions envy, curiosity, anxiety, and others are observed across time, they begin to reveal patterns about what draws attention, what generates motivation, and what feels personally meaningful.

The key shift lies in how these emotions are interpreted.

Instead of treating them as problems to eliminate, it can be more useful to treat them as clues to investigate.

What might this feeling be pointing toward? What value, interest, or concern does it reveal?

Approaching emotions with this kind of curiosity allows them to function as signals rather than obstacles.

8.3 Emotional Literacy

If emotions contain useful signals, the next challenge is learning how to interpret them.

Many people were never taught how to do this. In some environments emotions are treated as distractions, something to hide or control in order to appear rational and composed. Over time, this habit can lead people to ignore their emotional responses entirely.

But ignoring emotions does not eliminate them.

It only removes an important layer of information from one's understanding of experience.

Emotional literacy begins with a simple shift: recognizing emotions rather than immediately suppressing them. When a feeling appears whether it is excitement, frustration, curiosity, or anxiety the first step is simply to notice it.

What exactly am I feeling right now?

This question may seem obvious, but many people move through situations so quickly that they rarely pause to identify the emotion itself. A vague sense of tension may be interpreted as stress without examining whether it is actually anxiety, disappointment, or irritation.

Naming the emotion creates distance from it. Instead of being overwhelmed by the feeling, a person begins observing it.

The next step involves asking what the emotion might be pointing toward.

Every emotional reaction emerges in response to something a conversation, an expectation, a task, or an environment. When the emotion is examined carefully, it often reveals something about how that experience relates to personal values or priorities.

For example, frustration may signal that progress toward an important goal has been blocked. Curiosity may indicate that a topic resonates with one's interests. Anxiety may reveal that a situation carries uncertainty or importance.

These signals are not instructions. They do not automatically dictate what someone should do next. But they offer clues about what matters to the person experiencing them.

Developing emotional literacy also requires distinguishing between immediate reactions and deeper signals.

Some emotional responses are temporary. Fatigue after a long day may create irritability that fades with rest. A stressful situation may produce anxiety that disappears once the situation passes.

Other emotions appear repeatedly across different contexts.

A person may consistently feel energized when discussing certain topics. They may repeatedly experience frustration in particular environments. They may notice recurring curiosity about specific kinds of problems.

These patterns carry more reliable information than isolated emotional reactions.

Over time, awareness of these patterns begins to deepen.

A person who pays attention to their emotional responses across months or years may start recognizing connections between feelings, environments, and activities. Situations that once seemed confusing begin to make more sense. Emotional responses that once felt unpredictable begin to reveal consistent signals.

In this way, emotional literacy becomes a form of self-observation.

Rather than reacting automatically to each feeling, the individual learns to listen more carefully to what those feelings may be communicating.

As this skill develops, emotions become less like unpredictable disruptions and more like instruments that help interpret experience.

And through that interpretation, people often rediscover something important: the internal signals that point toward their own direction beneath the surrounding noise.

Part III

WHAT BURIES YOUR SIGNAL

Chapter 9

Fear

If internal signals exist signals of curiosity, energy, values, and emotional meaning why do so many people struggle to follow them?

Often the answer is not a lack of information.

It is fear.

Fear rarely appears as a dramatic barrier that announces itself openly. More often it operates quietly in the background of decision-making. A person may feel drawn toward exploring a new direction yet hesitate to act. They may sense that certain activities feel more aligned with who they are, but something prevents them from moving toward them.

The hesitation can appear practical or rational on the surface. Yet beneath many of these moments lies a simple emotional force: the desire to avoid loss, criticism, uncertainty, or regret.

Fear itself is not inherently harmful. It evolved to help human beings recognize danger and protect themselves from harm. In environments where survival was uncertain, this sensitivity to risk was essential.

But the environments in which modern decisions occur are rarely life-threatening. The risks people face today are more psychological than physical loss of status, embarrassment, social criticism, or uncertainty about the future.

When fear becomes attached to these experiences, it can quietly limit exploration.

A person may begin avoiding possibilities that carry even small amounts of uncertainty. Over time, the space for experimentation becomes narrower, and the signals that might reveal new directions are left unexplored.

Understanding how fear operates is therefore an important step in understanding why direction can feel so difficult to find.

9.1 Fear of Failure

Among the many forms of fear that influence human behavior, fear of failure is one of the most powerful.

Failure carries a particular weight in modern cultures. It is often interpreted not simply as an unsuccessful outcome but as a reflection of competence itself. When something goes wrong, the event can feel like evidence that a person lacks ability, judgment, or discipline.

This interpretation shapes behavior from an early age.

In many educational systems, success is defined primarily by correct answers. Students are rewarded for accuracy and penalized for mistakes. Exams measure how well someone avoids error, and performance is often summarized through grades that signal whether a student succeeded or failed.

Learning certainly requires structure and evaluation. But this environment can subtly teach an unintended lesson: that mistakes are signs of inadequacy rather than steps in the learning process.

As people move into professional life, similar patterns often continue.

Workplaces reward outcomes that appear efficient and successful. Promotions, recognition, and financial rewards tend to follow visible achievements. Failed projects, unsuccessful experiments, or ideas that did not work rarely receive the same attention.

In some cases, they carry reputational costs.

Because many forms of work occur in social environments, failure can feel particularly risky. An unsuccessful attempt is not only a personal disappointment; it may also become visible to colleagues, supervisors, or peers. The possibility of embarrassment or criticism can make the risk feel larger than the activity itself.

Over time, these experiences shape expectations.

People begin to internalize the belief that mistakes must be avoided whenever possible. They become cautious about attempting things they cannot guarantee they will succeed at. Before pursuing an unfamiliar path, they may wait until they feel fully prepared, fully qualified, or completely certain.

This mindset can feel responsible and rational.

But it carries an unintended consequence.

Exploration becomes difficult.

Many meaningful directions cannot be discovered through careful planning alone. They emerge through trial, adjustment, and experimentation. A person may need to attempt activities that do not work before recognizing which ones feel aligned with their interests and abilities.

When mistakes are treated as unacceptable, those experiments never occur.

A person may avoid exploring a new skill because they fear appearing inexperienced. Someone might hesitate to pursue a creative interest because early attempts may not be impressive. Another might remain in a stable but unsatisfying role because trying something different carries the possibility of failure.

In this way, fear of failure does not simply prevent mistakes.

It prevents discovery.

The irony is that many forms of expertise develop through repeated encounters with failure. Scientists test ideas that do not work before discovering those that do. Entrepreneurs build projects that collapse before understanding which models succeed. Artists create many imperfect works before producing pieces that resonate deeply.

Failure, in these cases, is not the opposite of progress.

It is part of the process that produces it.

Recognizing this does not eliminate the discomfort that mistakes can create. But it reframes their meaning.

Instead of viewing failure as evidence of inadequacy, it becomes possible to see it as information feedback about what works, what does not, and where alignment may or may not exist.

From that perspective, mistakes are not merely obstacles.

They are often the conditions through which direction becomes visible.

9.2 Fear of Judgment

Alongside the fear of failure, another force often shapes human behavior: the fear of judgment.

Most people do not make decisions in isolation. Their choices exist within networks of relationships family, friends, colleagues, and communities. These social environments provide support and connection, but they also create expectations about what kinds of decisions are acceptable.

Because human beings are deeply social creatures, the reactions of others carry significant psychological weight. Approval can feel reassuring, while criticism or disapproval can feel threatening. Even when no one explicitly expresses judgment, the possibility that it might occur can quietly influence behavior.

Consider how often people imagine the reactions of others before making a decision.

Someone thinking about changing careers may wonder how their family will interpret the move. A person considering a creative pursuit might worry about whether friends will see it as unrealistic. Another may hesitate to express an unconventional opinion in a professional environment because it could affect how colleagues perceive them.

These concerns rarely appear as direct prohibitions.

Instead, they appear as internal questions.

What will people think if I do this? Will others see this as a mistake? Will I appear irresponsible or confused?

Because reputation carries social consequences, these questions can become powerful influences.

Over time, many individuals begin organizing their lives around what appears respectable or acceptable to others. They pursue careers that are widely recognized as successful. They maintain identities that are already understood within their communities. Paths that might provoke confusion or criticism are quietly set aside.

In this way, fear of judgment can reinforce conformity.

The pressure is not always explicit. Often it operates through subtle signals admiration for certain achievements, silence toward unconventional choices, or casual comments that imply what a responsible life should look like.

When these signals accumulate, the desire for approval can gradually replace internal guidance.

A person may ignore curiosity about a different field because it does not match the expectations surrounding them. Another may continue pursuing goals that once seemed meaningful simply because others now associate them with that identity.

From the outside, these decisions can appear rational. They maintain stability and protect reputation.

But they can also silence internal signals.

The mind begins filtering possibilities not according to curiosity or energy, but according to anticipated reactions. Decisions become shaped by how they will be explained rather than by how they actually feel.

Recognizing this influence can be uncomfortable.

It requires acknowledging that many choices may have been shaped partly by the desire to avoid criticism or maintain approval.

But this recognition also opens a useful question:

How often do your decisions reflect what feels meaningful to you and how often do they reflect what you believe others expect?

Reflecting on that question can reveal how strongly the fear of judgment has influenced the path you have followed.

9.3 Fear of Uncertainty

Beyond failure and judgment lies another form of fear that shapes many decisions: the fear of uncertainty.

Human beings tend to prefer situations where outcomes are predictable. When the future appears clear, planning becomes easier. Expectations can be formed, risks can be estimated, and effort feels more manageable because the direction seems stable.

Uncertainty disrupts this sense of stability.

When outcomes are unclear, the mind struggles to form a reliable picture of what lies ahead. Questions multiply. Possibilities branch into different directions. The absence of clear answers can produce a low but persistent form of anxiety.

What if this decision leads nowhere? What if the effort does not produce the result I expect? What if I discover too late that I chose the wrong path?

These questions rarely have immediate solutions.

Part of the discomfort of uncertainty comes from the way human cognition works. The mind is designed to reduce ambiguity whenever possible. It searches for patterns, predictions, and explanations that transform unknown situations into understandable ones.

When those patterns are missing, tension appears.

One common response to this tension is the search for guarantees.

Before acting, people often try to gather enough information to ensure that their decision will succeed. They research options, compare alternatives, and analyze possible outcomes. They seek advice from others who appear more certain or experienced.

This process can be useful.

Information and reflection help people make thoughtful choices. But the search for certainty can also become endless. When the standard for action becomes complete confidence, movement becomes difficult.

Many meaningful directions cannot be approached with guarantees.

Consider someone exploring a new field of work. They cannot know in advance whether the environment will suit them. A person developing a creative project cannot be certain how others will respond. Someone considering a change in life direction cannot predict every consequence of that choice.

In each case, discovery requires entering territory where outcomes remain uncertain.

Yet the desire for certainty often encourages delay.

A person may tell themselves they will act once they have more information, once conditions become clearer, or once they feel completely prepared. In the meantime, months or years can pass while possibilities remain theoretical rather than experienced.

The difficulty is that clarity often emerges only after action has begun.

Many people discover what they value not through analysis alone, but through engagement with real situations. They learn which environments energize them by working within those environments. They discover which activities resonate with their interests by trying them.

In other words, understanding often follows exploration rather than preceding it.

Uncertainty, therefore, is not simply an obstacle to direction.

It is often a condition of genuine discovery.

9.4 How Fear Freezes Exploration

When fear becomes attached to failure, judgment, and uncertainty, it begins to shape behavior in predictable ways.

One of the most common responses to fear is avoidance.

The human nervous system is designed to reduce exposure to situations that appear threatening. When something feels risky or uncomfortable, attention shifts toward ways of minimizing that risk. The person delays action, chooses safer alternatives, or remains within environments that feel familiar.

In situations involving physical danger, this response is useful. Avoidance protects the body from harm.

But when the perceived threat is psychological rather than physical criticism, embarrassment, uncertainty about outcomes the same mechanism can quietly limit exploration.

A person may sense curiosity about a new direction but hesitate to act because the outcome is unclear. Another may feel drawn toward creative work but avoid sharing it publicly because the possibility of criticism feels uncomfortable. Someone else may remain in a stable but unsatisfying environment simply because it feels safer than attempting something unfamiliar.

Over time, this pattern creates a narrowing effect.

The individual begins choosing environments where expectations are known and risks appear manageable. Familiar routines replace experimentation. Decisions prioritize stability rather than discovery.

From the outside, this behavior can appear responsible or cautious. In many cases it is. Stability and careful decision-making are important aspects of a functioning life.

But when avoidance becomes the dominant strategy, curiosity begins to fade.

Fear narrows attention.

Instead of imagining possibilities, the mind becomes preoccupied with potential negative outcomes. Instead of asking what might be interesting or meaningful to explore, the person asks what might go wrong.

Imagination contracts. Exploration slows.

Eventually, a person may feel stuck not because opportunities do not exist, but because fear has quietly restricted the range of possibilities they feel comfortable pursuing.

Breaking this pattern rarely requires dramatic changes.

In many cases, exploration can begin through small experiments.

A person curious about writing does not need to abandon their current work immediately; they might begin by writing regularly in private. Someone interested in a different field might take a course, volunteer, or speak with people working in that environment. A person considering a career shift might begin exploring related skills while maintaining their existing responsibilities.

These small experiments reduce the psychological cost of uncertainty.

Instead of confronting a single high-stakes decision, the person gathers information through experience. Each experiment produces feedback about what feels engaging, what feels draining, and what might deserve further attention.

Gradually, fear loses some of its influence.

The unfamiliar becomes slightly more familiar. The imagined risks become clearer, and many of them turn out to be smaller than they once appeared.

Recognizing the presence of fear does not eliminate it entirely. Fear is a natural part of human psychology.

But understanding how it operates allows people to relate to it differently.

Instead of allowing fear to quietly freeze exploration, it becomes possible to notice its influence and begin moving forward in small ways despite it.

Chapter 10

Borrowed Ambitions

Not every ambition begins as a personal decision.

Many goals enter a person's life quietly, long before they are consciously examined. They appear through conversations, expectations, cultural messages, and the examples provided by others. Over time, these influences accumulate until certain directions begin to feel obvious or inevitable.

A student grows up hearing that particular professions are respectable. A family celebrates specific achievements. Schools reward certain kinds of performance. Society repeatedly presents images of what a successful life should look like.

Gradually, ambitions take shape.

The person begins striving toward outcomes that seem meaningful because they have been described that way for years. Educational paths, career milestones, and life structures appear widely accepted and admired, making them feel like natural destinations.

None of this is necessarily harmful.

External expectations can provide guidance and structure. They help people navigate complex environments and offer models for stability and achievement.

But sometimes these ambitions are not entirely one's own.

A person may spend years pursuing goals that once seemed important, only to discover that the motivation behind them feels strangely distant. The achievement arrives, yet the satisfaction feels muted or incomplete.

In such moments, a difficult question can emerge:

Whose ambition was this?

Understanding borrowed ambitions requires examining where our goals come from. Many aspirations originate not in personal curiosity or internal alignment, but in the expectations that surround a person from an early age.

Recognizing this influence is not about rejecting every external influence. It is about learning to distinguish between ambitions that genuinely belong to us and those we have inherited without noticing.

10.1 Family Expectations

For most people, the first ideas about success come from family.

Long before individuals make conscious decisions about their future, they observe how the adults around them think about work, stability, and reputation. These ideas are rarely presented as formal instructions. Instead, they appear through everyday conversation, small comments, and the examples that families celebrate or worry about.

A child might hear that certain professions are respectable and reliable. Another might notice that particular achievements high grades, prestigious universities, secure careers receive strong approval. Over time, these signals accumulate.

Without deliberate intention, a picture of the future begins to form.

Parents often encourage paths they believe will provide safety and stability. If they experienced economic uncertainty, they may emphasize careers that appear financially secure. If they value social reputation, they may guide their children toward professions associated with prestige or respect.

In many cases, these expectations come from care rather than pressure.

Families want their children to avoid unnecessary hardship. They want them to succeed in environments that appear predictable and rewarding. From that perspective, encouraging certain ambitions can feel like responsible guidance.

Yet even gentle guidance can shape imagination.

A child who repeatedly hears that medicine, law, engineering, or business represent successful futures may gradually internalize those ideas. By the time they begin making independent decisions, those paths already feel familiar. They appear less like external expectations and more like natural possibilities.

Because these ambitions were learned early, they often feel like one's own.

A student may pursue a demanding academic path without ever pausing to ask why it seems necessary. Another may aim for a particular career because it has always been described as the logical next step.

Sometimes the alignment is genuine. The person's interests and abilities may truly match the direction their family encouraged.

But in other cases, the connection is weaker.

A person might discover that the activities required by the path daily responsibilities, modes of thinking, or professional environments do not resonate with their natural tendencies. Yet stepping away from that direction can feel difficult because the ambition carries emotional significance for the family.

Family pride can reinforce the path.

Parents express pride when their child progresses along a respected trajectory. Relatives share the news of achievements. These responses create powerful emotional incentives to continue moving forward.

At the same time, family fears can also influence decisions.

A parent who worries about financial insecurity may discourage careers that appear unpredictable. Another who values stability may caution against paths involving risk or creative uncertainty. Even when these concerns are expressed gently, they can shape how a person evaluates their options.

As a result, individuals sometimes inherit ambitions without fully noticing.

The goals feel familiar because they were present throughout childhood. They carry emotional weight because they are connected to family identity and approval.

None of this makes inherited ambitions inherently wrong.

Family expectations can provide direction during early life when experience is limited. They can encourage discipline, responsibility, and persistence.

But they can also narrow exploration.

When certain paths are treated as the only acceptable options, curiosity about other possibilities may remain unexplored.

Recognizing this influence does not require rejecting family values. It simply invites a careful question:

Which of my ambitions genuinely reflect my own interests and which ones began as expectations that I learned long ago?

10.2 Prestige Paths

Beyond family influence, another force often shapes ambition: prestige.

In every society, certain professions and achievements acquire symbolic value. They become associated with intelligence, competence, influence, or success. Over time, these roles are not only understood as forms of work but as markers of status.

When someone says they are a doctor, lawyer, engineer, executive, or entrepreneur, the title often carries meaning beyond the work itself. It signals capability, education, and social recognition.

These signals are powerful.

Prestige functions almost like a social shortcut. Instead of examining the details of a person's work, people rely on the reputation attached to the role. The profession itself becomes a symbol of achievement.

For individuals deciding what to pursue, this symbolism can be highly attractive.

A student may gravitate toward a prestigious path not only because of genuine interest, but also because the role carries recognition. Friends and family respond with admiration. Society treats the profession as evidence of success.

In this way, prestige can become a motivating force.

The pursuit of recognition can provide direction, discipline, and a sense of progress. Achieving a respected position often brings financial stability, professional networks, and opportunities that might otherwise remain inaccessible.

But prestige can also obscure a deeper question.

Does the daily reality of the work actually fit the person pursuing it?

From a distance, a prestigious career may appear highly desirable. Yet every role contains specific demands long hours, particular kinds of thinking, certain forms of responsibility, and environments that require specific psychological traits.

Someone drawn toward prestige may focus on the symbolic reward while paying less attention to the lived experience of the work itself.

For example, a profession admired for its influence may involve years of routine tasks before meaningful autonomy appears. A career associated with intellectual status may require sustained attention to technical details that not everyone enjoys. A role celebrated for its impact may involve constant pressure and responsibility that some individuals find exhausting.

When the symbolic image of the career differs from its daily reality, a quiet mismatch can emerge.

A person may achieve the status they once pursued only to discover that the work itself does not produce engagement or satisfaction. The external recognition remains, but the internal connection feels weaker than expected.

This realization can be surprising.

From the outside, the person appears successful. The achievement that once represented ambition has been reached. Yet internally, the sense of alignment that was expected to accompany that achievement may not appear.

Prestige, in other words, does not guarantee fulfillment.

It provides recognition, but recognition alone cannot determine whether a particular path resonates with a person's natural interests, energy patterns, and values.

Recognizing this does not mean that prestigious paths are inherently misaligned. Many people genuinely enjoy and thrive within them.

But it does raise an important question:

Is the attraction coming from the work itself, or from the status associated with it?

And perhaps more importantly:

Does this form of prestige actually align with the internal signals that guide your own direction?

10.3 Social Success Definitions

Beyond family expectations and prestigious careers lies a broader influence: society's shared definitions of success.

Every culture develops visible markers that signal whether a person is progressing well in life. These markers often appear in recognizable forms financial wealth, professional status, public recognition, influence, or visible accomplishments.

Because these signals are widely understood, they become convenient benchmarks.

When someone earns more money, receives a promotion, gains followers, publishes work, or reaches positions of authority, these achievements are easily recognized as signs of success. They provide clear evidence that a person is moving upward according to widely accepted standards.

Over time, these benchmarks become so familiar that they begin to feel natural.

People rarely stop to ask why wealth, recognition, or influence carry such strong symbolic meaning. Instead, they absorb the assumption that these outcomes represent progress. The goals become part of the background structure through which individuals evaluate their own lives.

This process often happens quietly.

A young professional may pursue promotions without questioning why the hierarchy feels important. Someone may measure their worth through income or recognition simply because these indicators are repeatedly presented as meaningful. Social media can amplify this effect by constantly displaying visible milestones awards, achievements, travel, property, or influence.

When these images accumulate, they reinforce the idea that a successful life follows a particular trajectory.

The difficulty is not that these achievements lack value.

Financial stability can provide freedom and security. Recognition can create opportunities. Influence can allow people to shape ideas or institutions.

The difficulty arises when these external markers become the only measures of success.

When that happens, individuals may begin pursuing outcomes that appear impressive without examining whether those outcomes actually resonate with their internal values or interests.

A person might spend years striving for status within an organization, only to discover that the responsibilities attached to that position feel exhausting rather than meaningful. Another may focus on accumulating visible achievements while feeling increasingly detached from the activities required to produce them.

From the outside, these lives may appear highly successful.

But internally, the connection between effort and meaning may feel surprisingly weak.

This disconnect can be confusing because external success is supposed to bring satisfaction. When it does not, people may assume the problem lies in themselves that they should simply work harder or achieve more.

Yet sometimes the problem lies in the definition of success itself.

External benchmarks can be useful signals, but they do not necessarily reflect the deeper patterns that shape a person's internal direction.

Recognizing this creates an opportunity to reconsider an important question:

When you think about success, whose definition are you using?

And what would success look like if it were defined not only by external recognition, but also by alignment with your own curiosity, energy, and values?

10.4 Recognizing What Isn't Yours

Once a person begins to understand how family expectations, prestige, and social definitions of success shape ambition, an important question naturally follows:

Which of my goals genuinely belong to me?

This question is not always easy to answer. Ambitions that originate from external influences often feel deeply familiar because they have been present for so long. A career path may have been encouraged since childhood. A particular idea of success may have been repeated by teachers, mentors, or cultural narratives for years.

When these influences are absorbed early, they can feel indistinguishable from personal desire.

Recognizing borrowed ambitions therefore requires careful reflection on where one's goals first came from.

When you imagine a particular future an occupation, a lifestyle, a level of recognition what originally made that outcome seem important? Was it driven by sustained curiosity and engagement, or by admiration and approval from others?

Sometimes the answer becomes visible through motivation.

Certain ambitions are sustained primarily by external validation. A person may feel driven when others express admiration or when visible progress earns recognition. But when that recognition disappears, the motivation fades as well.

Other ambitions behave differently.

Even when recognition is absent, the activity itself continues to hold interest. A person remains curious about the subject, continues thinking about it outside formal obligations, and feels engaged in the process rather than only in the outcome.

This difference between approval and engagement can reveal important clues.

Another useful observation involves the emotional tone surrounding a goal.

Some ambitions feel like obligations. They carry a sense of responsibility something that must be achieved in order to meet expectations or maintain a certain identity. Effort is driven by duty rather than genuine interest.

Other ambitions feel more exploratory.

Even when they require effort and uncertainty, they create a sense of curiosity or energy. The person feels drawn toward them rather than pushed from behind.

These distinctions often become clearer when patterns are observed across time.

A person may notice that certain pursuits consistently feel heavy, as though they are being carried out to maintain a narrative of success. At the same time, other interests continue to reappear quietly in different forms, even when they are not rewarded or encouraged.

Gradually, these observations allow a kind of filtering process to begin.

Some goals begin to lose their emotional weight once their origins are understood. They may still be respected or appreciated, but they no longer feel necessary to pursue.

Other interests, once overlooked or dismissed, may start to appear more significant.

This process does not require rejecting every external influence. Guidance from family, mentors, or culture can still provide valuable insight.

The important step is simply recognizing which ambitions were inherited and which ones arise from genuine alignment.

When borrowed ambitions are identified, something subtle begins to change.

The space they once occupied in the mind becomes available again.

And within that space, more authentic directions often begin to emerge.

Chapter 11

The Productivity Trap

In many modern environments, productivity has become one of the primary measures of personal value.

People are encouraged to work efficiently, manage their time carefully, and produce visible results. Productivity tools promise greater organization, faster execution, and improved performance. Books, podcasts, and professional advice often emphasize strategies for doing more in less time.

At first glance, this focus appears entirely reasonable. Productivity helps individuals and organizations function effectively. It allows people to complete responsibilities, pursue goals, and contribute to the systems they participate in.

But over time, something subtle can happen.

The emphasis on productivity begins to shift from a practical tool into a measure of personal worth.

A person may begin evaluating themselves according to how much they accomplish. Days filled with activity feel successful. Periods of rest, uncertainty, or reflection may start to feel uncomfortable or even irresponsible.

Gradually, the pace of life accelerates.

Tasks multiply, schedules fill, and productivity becomes a constant background expectation. People remain busy, moving continuously from one obligation to the next.

Yet beneath this constant activity, an important question can remain unanswered:

Is all of this effort actually moving in a meaningful direction?

Understanding the productivity trap requires examining how busyness, achievement, and constant optimization can quietly replace something essential the time and attention needed to reflect on what truly matters.

11.1 Busyness as Identity

One of the most visible features of modern life is the constant presence of activity.

Calendars fill quickly. Messages arrive continuously. Meetings, tasks, and deadlines organize the rhythm of the day. For many people, the experience of being busy has become so normal that it rarely invites reflection.

In fact, busyness is often admired.

When someone asks how things are going, a common response is simply, "I've been very busy." The statement is rarely interpreted as a complaint. Instead, it often functions as a subtle signal that the person's time is valuable and their work is important.

In this way, busyness becomes a marker of significance.

A person who manages many responsibilities appears productive and engaged. A full schedule suggests commitment, competence, and relevance. Even outside professional settings, people sometimes measure their own effectiveness by how much they manage to accomplish within a limited amount of time.

Over time, this pattern can shape identity.

People begin describing themselves through the activities that occupy their days. Conversations revolve around projects, deadlines, and obligations. Personal worth becomes intertwined with visible productivity.

Someone might say, "Work has been overwhelming lately," but the tone carries a hint of pride. The pressure itself becomes evidence that the person is needed.

This cultural admiration for busyness reinforces the pattern.

Professional environments often reward visible activity. Quick responses to messages signal attentiveness. A crowded calendar can appear as evidence of importance. Individuals who seem constantly engaged may be perceived as more dedicated than those who move at a slower pace, even when the actual results are similar.

Over time, the experience of busyness can become self-reinforcing.

When people feel uncertain about their direction, activity can provide a temporary sense of clarity. Completing tasks produces visible progress. Checking items off a list creates the impression of movement. The schedule fills with obligations that prevent long pauses for reflection.

In this sense, busyness can function as a form of protection.

Remaining constantly occupied reduces the need to ask deeper questions about whether the work itself is meaningful. As long as there is always something to do, the underlying direction of those efforts can remain unexamined.

A person may move efficiently from one responsibility to the next, maintaining a high level of productivity while still feeling unsure about where their efforts ultimately lead.

From the outside, the life appears active and successful.

But activity alone does not guarantee direction.

Busyness can create the appearance of progress even when the movement itself is circular. Without reflection, constant activity may simply produce more activity.

Being busy, in other words, does not necessarily mean that one is moving toward something meaningful.

11.2 Achievement Addiction

Busyness often leads naturally to another dynamic: the pursuit of achievement.

Achievements provide clear signals of progress. A project is completed. A promotion is earned. A milestone is reached. In many environments these moments are accompanied by recognition from others praise from colleagues, approval from family, or visible markers of advancement.

These responses create a powerful emotional effect.

When effort results in recognition, the mind experiences a sense of reward. Confidence rises. The person feels capable, validated, and temporarily certain that their work matters. In uncertain environments, these moments of affirmation can feel especially meaningful.

There is nothing inherently problematic about this response. Human motivation is closely tied to feedback, and recognition helps individuals understand that their efforts are producing results.

The difficulty emerges when achievement itself becomes the primary source of validation.

If a person's sense of worth begins to depend heavily on visible accomplishments, each success quickly creates the desire for another. After reaching one milestone, attention shifts almost immediately toward the next. A completed project is followed by a new target. A promotion leads to the pursuit of a higher role.

From the outside, this pattern can appear admirable.

The person looks driven and ambitious. Their list of accomplishments grows steadily. They remain in constant motion, moving from one achievement to another.

But internally the experience can feel different.

The satisfaction produced by each accomplishment often fades surprisingly quickly. What initially felt like a meaningful victory becomes ordinary once it is achieved. The mind adapts to the new level of success and begins searching for the next source of validation.

Psychologists sometimes describe this pattern as a form of reward adaptation. The brain quickly adjusts to new achievements, reducing their emotional impact and encouraging the pursuit of another reward.

Over time, this cycle can begin to resemble addiction.

Not in the sense of physical dependency, but in the psychological pattern of repeatedly seeking the same emotional reinforcement. The lift produced by achievement becomes something to chase. Without new accomplishments, a person may begin to feel restless or uncertain about their value.

Gradually, achievement becomes part of identity.

Instead of asking what activities feel meaningful or aligned, the individual focuses on which goals will produce the next measurable success. The question quietly shifts from

What work fits me best?

to

What achievement will confirm my competence next?

Over time, this orientation can create a subtle disconnection.

A person may continue accumulating accomplishments while feeling increasingly uncertain about whether those achievements actually reflect their deeper interests or values. The goals remain impressive, yet the connection between the activity and the person pursuing it becomes less clear.

This does not mean achievement itself is problematic. Accomplishments can represent real growth, contribution, and progress.

The deeper question is simply whether those achievements reflect genuine alignment or whether they have become a substitute for it.

Because an important question often remains beneath the surface:

Does achievement always indicate that a person is moving in the right direction?

11.3 Optimization Replacing Reflection

Alongside the pursuit of productivity and achievement, another modern habit has quietly taken hold: optimization.

In many professional and personal environments, people are encouraged to continuously improve how they manage their time and attention. Books promise better systems for organizing tasks. Applications track habits, schedules, and performance. Advice columns offer strategies for maximizing focus, reducing distractions, and squeezing more efficiency out of each day.

At one level, these tools can be helpful.

Organizing work more effectively can reduce unnecessary stress. Clear systems can prevent tasks from being forgotten and allow people to manage complex responsibilities. In environments where demands are high, a certain degree of efficiency is necessary.

The difficulty arises when optimization itself becomes the central goal.

Instead of asking whether their activities are meaningful, people begin asking how those activities can be performed faster and more efficiently. The emphasis shifts from *what* someone is doing to *how efficiently* it is done.

This shift is subtle.

A person might carefully design their morning routine, track their work output, and analyze how each hour of the day is spent. They optimize their calendar, refine their task lists, and experiment with systems intended to increase productivity.

But rarely do these systems ask a more fundamental question:

Why are these particular tasks worth optimizing in the first place?

Efficiency can easily become detached from purpose.

Someone might become extremely skilled at managing tasks that were never carefully chosen. They complete obligations faster, respond more quickly, and move through their schedule with impressive discipline yet the underlying direction of their work remains unexamined.

In this way, optimization can quietly replace reflection.

Reflection requires a different mental pace. It involves stepping away from immediate tasks and considering broader questions about direction, meaning, and alignment. These questions cannot usually be answered quickly. They often emerge through slower, quieter forms of thinking during long walks, unstructured conversations, or moments when attention is not dominated by immediate demands.

Yet modern environments rarely encourage this kind of pause.

When every hour is expected to produce measurable output, reflection can begin to feel like wasted time. Silence becomes uncomfortable. Unscheduled moments appear inefficient.

But without reflection, efficiency alone cannot guide direction.

A person may become highly effective at executing tasks while remaining uncertain about whether those tasks truly matter to them.

Discovering genuine direction requires more than doing things well.

It requires stepping back from constant optimization long enough to consider whether the work itself is aligned with one's deeper interests, values, and patterns of energy.

In other words, reflection is not the opposite of productivity.

It is often the condition that allows meaningful direction to emerge in the first place.

11.4 Movement vs Growth

One of the central confusions within the productivity trap is the tendency to treat movement as evidence of growth.

Movement is easy to recognize. Tasks are completed, meetings are attended, messages are answered, and goals are pursued. A person moves quickly from one responsibility to another, often maintaining a full schedule and a steady stream of visible output.

From the outside, this activity looks like progress.

But movement and growth are not the same.

Movement describes activity. It measures how much is happening. Growth, by contrast, describes change in understanding, capability, or direction. It reflects whether a person's actions are gradually shaping a life that feels more aligned with their values and interests.

It is possible to experience a great deal of movement without experiencing much growth.

A person might spend years advancing through a series of tasks and promotions while feeling internally unchanged. The responsibilities become larger, the schedule becomes more demanding, and the achievements accumulate. Yet the deeper questions about meaning, curiosity, or alignment remain unresolved.

Movement continues, but growth is uncertain.

In many cases, constant activity can even serve as a way of avoiding deeper reflection.

When schedules are full and responsibilities are immediate, there is little time to pause and examine whether the direction of one's effort truly makes sense. Activity creates momentum, and momentum can make it easier to continue moving forward than to step back and reconsider the path itself.

This avoidance is rarely intentional.

A person may simply follow the natural rhythm of obligations and opportunities. Each decision leads to the next, and the structure of the environment encourages continuous forward motion.

Yet occasionally a quieter moment appears.

Perhaps during a vacation, a period of transition, or an unexpected pause in routine, a person may notice a subtle uncertainty. Despite years of movement, they may wonder whether their efforts have actually led them closer to something meaningful.

These moments of reflection can feel uncomfortable because they interrupt the familiar rhythm of activity.

But they can also be valuable.

Growth often requires slowing down long enough to observe what constant motion tends to obscure. When the pace of activity decreases, patterns become easier to notice. Certain tasks feel aligned with one's interests and values, while others reveal themselves as obligations that no longer feel meaningful.

Through this process, movement begins to separate from growth.

Movement asks how much is being done.

Growth asks whether what is being done is actually shaping a direction that feels true.

Recognizing this difference can change how a person approaches their time and effort. Instead of measuring success purely through activity, they begin asking whether their actions contribute to deeper understanding, alignment, or development.

Because genuine growth rarely emerges from motion alone.

It emerges when movement is guided by intentional direction.

Chapter 12

Identity Rigidity

As people move through life, they gradually construct identities.

These identities form through education, work, relationships, and the roles individuals take on within their communities. Someone becomes a student, then a professional, perhaps a specialist in a particular field. Another becomes known as the reliable friend, the ambitious colleague, the creative thinker, or the practical decision-maker.

Over time, these roles begin to solidify.

Others come to associate the person with certain abilities and expectations. Introductions reinforce the identity: *She is a lawyer. He works in finance. They are an entrepreneur.* The description becomes a convenient shorthand for understanding who someone is.

At first, identities serve a useful purpose. They help organize social life and provide a sense of direction. They allow individuals to develop expertise, build relationships, and create stable structures for their lives.

But identities can also become rigid.

Roles that once felt meaningful may gradually begin to feel less aligned with a person's evolving interests or values. Curiosity shifts. New questions emerge. A person may begin to feel drawn toward different kinds of work, learning, or ways of living.

Yet despite these internal changes, many individuals continue along the same path.

Part of the difficulty lies in how identity becomes intertwined with commitment. When a role has been built through years of effort, stepping away from it can feel like abandoning a significant part of one's life story.

As a result, people sometimes remain attached to identities long after those identities have stopped fitting comfortably.

To understand why this happens, we must examine several psychological forces that quietly reinforce identity rigidity.

A person may spend a decade building a career that once felt exciting, only to realize that the identity they worked so hard to establish no longer reflects who they have become.

12.1 Sunk-Cost Thinking

One of the strongest forces that keeps people attached to an identity is the weight of past investment.

Over time, individuals invest enormous amounts of energy into building a particular path. Years of education, professional training, relationships within a field, and the gradual development of expertise all contribute to a sense of commitment. The longer someone has followed a certain direction, the more it begins to feel irreversible.

Psychologists often describe this pattern as the *sunk-cost effect.* When people invest significant time, effort, or resources into something, they feel a strong pressure to continue even when the original choice no longer feels like the best option.

In practical terms, the reasoning often sounds familiar.

Someone who spent years studying a specialized subject may feel obligated to remain in that field. A professional who has built a reputation in a particular industry may hesitate to explore other interests because doing so might appear to waste the years already invested.

The thought appears quietly but persistently:

I've already put too much into this to change direction now.

From a purely logical perspective, this reasoning is flawed. Past investments cannot be recovered whether a person continues or changes course. The time spent acquiring skills or knowledge remains part of their experience regardless of what comes next.

Yet the emotional weight of those investments is powerful.

People often feel the need to justify earlier decisions not only to others but to themselves. Admitting that a path no longer fits can feel like admitting that previous effort was misguided. Even when circumstances have changed, the person may feel compelled to remain consistent with the past.

This pressure can quietly lock someone into roles that no longer feel aligned.

Imagine a person who spent a decade training for a demanding profession. At first the work felt meaningful, but over time their interests shifted. They become curious about different kinds of problems or environments. Yet leaving the profession feels almost impossible, because doing so would appear to invalidate years of preparation.

Another person may have built a business or career that once represented an exciting opportunity. As responsibilities grow, however, the work begins to feel draining rather than energizing. Still, the thought of abandoning the path feels unthinkable because so much effort has already been invested.

In both cases, the individual remains committed not because the direction still fits, but because the past exerts psychological gravity.

The sunk-cost effect narrows imagination.

Instead of asking what direction might feel most aligned today, the person focuses on protecting earlier investments. Exploration becomes difficult because every alternative seems to threaten the value of what has already been done.

Yet experience does not lose its value simply because direction changes.

Skills, knowledge, and relationships developed in one context often transfer in unexpected ways to another. The past remains part of a person's story regardless of where the future leads.

Recognizing the sunk-cost effect does not mean abandoning commitments impulsively. Many paths require persistence through difficult periods.

But it does invite a different perspective.

The years already invested in a path are part of your history, not a contract that must determine the rest of your life.

Past investments can inform your direction but they do not have to define it.

12.2 Fear of Reinvention

Even when a person begins to sense that their current path no longer fits, another force often appears: the fear of reinvention.

Changing direction rarely involves only practical adjustments. It often requires altering the story that others and sometimes the individual themselves have come to believe about who they are. A person who has spent years being known as one thing may suddenly consider becoming something else.

This shift can feel unsettling.

In many environments, consistency is quietly valued. Stability signals reliability, and long-term commitment to a single path is often interpreted as evidence of discipline or seriousness. When someone changes direction, the decision can disrupt these expectations.

Friends, colleagues, or family members may react with surprise.

Why leave a stable career? Why start again in a different field? Why step away from something that seemed to be working?

Even when these questions are asked with curiosity rather than criticism, they can create pressure. The individual considering a change may feel that they must justify their decision in ways that make sense to others.

Reinvention can also affect credibility.

A person who has built expertise in one domain may feel confident and respected within that environment. But stepping into a new area often means becoming a beginner again. Skills must be rebuilt, knowledge must be expanded, and reputation must be developed from the beginning.

This transition can feel like a loss of status.

Someone who once spoke with authority may now find themselves asking basic questions. The identity that once provided confidence becomes less stable, and the person may worry that others will see them as uncertain or inconsistent.

Beyond social concerns, reinvention also introduces psychological uncertainty.

Familiar roles provide structure. They define routines, relationships, and expectations. When those structures change, the future becomes less predictable. The person may not know exactly how the new direction will unfold or whether it will succeed.

For this reason, many individuals remain in roles that feel increasingly misaligned.

The identity may no longer reflect who they are becoming, but it still provides a sense of security. Remaining on the established path feels easier than entering a period of uncertainty where outcomes cannot be guaranteed.

Yet reinvention has always been part of human development.

Interests evolve as people encounter new experiences. Skills develop that open unexpected possibilities. Questions that once felt settled begin to reappear with new meaning.

When these internal signals shift, the identity built around earlier circumstances may no longer fit comfortably.

At such moments, reinvention is not necessarily a sign of instability.

It may simply be a response to new information about who a person is becoming.

12.3 Loyalty to Past Selves

Another force that sustains identity rigidity is loyalty to earlier versions of oneself.

At different stages of life, people make decisions that reflect who they are at that moment. A student chooses a field of study. A young professional commits to a particular career path. Someone adopts certain beliefs about what kind of work they value or what kind of person they want to become.

These choices are rarely random.

They are shaped by the experiences, knowledge, and opportunities available at the time. When a person commits to a direction early in life, the decision often feels meaningful and deliberate. It becomes part of their emerging identity.

Over time, however, individuals continue to change.

New experiences expand their understanding of the world. Exposure to different environments introduces new possibilities. Interests evolve, and values sometimes shift in ways that were difficult to anticipate earlier.

Despite these changes, the earlier identity often remains.

Part of the reason is the social expectation of consistency. People are frequently encouraged to remain loyal to the decisions they have made. Changing direction can appear inconsistent, and inconsistency is sometimes interpreted as uncertainty or lack of discipline.

As a result, individuals may feel pressure to remain aligned with choices made years earlier.

Someone who once declared a strong commitment to a particular field may continue pursuing it even when their curiosity has moved elsewhere.

Another person may hold onto beliefs or ambitions that once felt deeply important, even though their current perspective has changed.

In these situations, the tension between past and present becomes visible.

Growth naturally produces new questions and interests. Yet the identity formed around earlier commitments continues exerting influence. The person may feel as though they are betraying their former self by reconsidering the path they once chose.

Psychologists sometimes describe this phenomenon as a form of psychological inertia.

Just as physical objects resist changes in motion, identities built over time tend to resist change as well. The longer a person has held a particular role or self-definition, the more stable it feels. Altering that identity requires energy, reflection, and often a willingness to tolerate uncertainty.

This inertia can slow personal change even when internal signals begin pointing in new directions.

A person may recognize that their interests have evolved but continue acting according to the expectations attached to their earlier identity. The result is a gradual mismatch between who they once were and who they are becoming.

Recognizing this pattern can be liberating.

It allows individuals to see that loyalty to a past identity is not always necessary. Earlier decisions were made with the knowledge and perspective available at the time. As that knowledge changes, it becomes reasonable for direction to change as well.

Growth does not always require rejecting the past.

But it often requires loosening the attachment to identities that no longer reflect the person one has become.

In this way, personal development sometimes begins with a quiet but important step: allowing outdated self-definitions to fade so that new ones can emerge.

12.4 Identity as Evolving Process

One way to loosen the grip of identity rigidity is to reconsider what identity actually is.

Many people unconsciously treat identity as a fixed description. A person becomes something a profession, a role, a reputation and that label begins to define how both they and others understand who they are. Once established, the identity feels stable, almost permanent.

But human development rarely follows such a static model.

Throughout life, individuals pass through different stages of experience. Early interests are shaped by family and education. Young adulthood introduces new environments and responsibilities. Later years often bring different priorities, deeper reflection, and a broader perspective on what matters.

At each stage, the person changes.

New knowledge appears. Skills expand. Encounters with different people and ideas reshape how the world is understood. Interests that once seemed central may gradually fade, while new curiosities quietly emerge.

This evolution is natural.

Yet when identity is treated as something fixed, these changes can feel like contradictions. A person may worry that shifting interests mean they lack consistency. They may feel uneasy about reconsidering goals that once seemed certain.

A different framework offers a more realistic view.

Instead of seeing identity as a permanent label, it can be understood as an ongoing process. Each stage of life reveals new information about how a person thinks, what energizes them, and what they value. Identity develops gradually as these signals accumulate.

From this perspective, change is not a problem to be corrected.

It is evidence that the individual is continuing to learn about themselves.

A flexible identity allows adaptation.

Someone who once identified strongly with a particular profession can still appreciate that experience while remaining open to new directions. A person whose values have evolved can adjust their priorities without feeling that they are abandoning who they were before.

The earlier identity becomes part of a longer story rather than a rigid definition that must be preserved.

This perspective also reduces the fear often associated with change.

If identity is understood as a process rather than a fixed state, exploring new possibilities does not require discarding the past. It simply reflects the natural continuation of development. Each experience contributes new signals that help refine one's understanding of direction.

Over time, the person becomes less concerned with maintaining a single consistent label and more interested in following the patterns that continue to emerge through curiosity, energy, and reflection.

Seen in this way, identity is not something that must be protected from change.

It is something that unfolds.

And recognizing that unfolding can allow people to approach their lives with greater flexibility, curiosity, and openness to the signals that continue to shape who they are becoming.

Part IV

DISCOVERING YOUR SIGNAL

Chapter 13

Observing Attention

One of the most reliable signals of personal direction appears in a place people rarely examine carefully: their own attention.

Throughout the day, attention moves constantly. Thoughts drift from one subject to another. A person notices certain problems, ideas, conversations, or possibilities while ignoring countless others. In most cases this movement happens automatically, without deliberate intention.

Yet the patterns of attention are rarely random.

Over time, the mind tends to return to certain kinds of questions, topics, or observations. Some subjects repeatedly capture curiosity. Certain problems attract sustained thought. Other topics appear briefly but fade quickly from interest.

These patterns often reveal something deeper than momentary distraction.

They indicate where the mind naturally gravitates when it is not being directed by obligation or expectation. In that sense, attention acts as a quiet guide. It reflects the underlying structure of a person's curiosity, values, and intellectual interests.

Learning to observe these patterns can reveal signals that formal planning often overlooks.

Instead of asking abstract questions about what direction life should take, it can be more revealing to begin with a simpler inquiry: where does your attention consistently return when it is free to wander?

13.1 What Occupies Your Mind

One of the simplest ways to begin understanding attention is to observe what the mind returns to when it is free.

During moments without immediate demands while walking, waiting, commuting, or resting thoughts begin to wander. The mind moves from one idea to another, exploring possibilities, replaying conversations, imagining solutions, or reflecting on questions that have no immediate answer.

At first, these thoughts may appear random.

But when they are observed over time, patterns often begin to emerge.

Some people notice that their minds repeatedly return to practical problems. They may find themselves analyzing how systems work, thinking about how organizations could operate more efficiently, or considering ways to solve logistical challenges.

Others notice that their attention gravitates toward human experiences. They may replay conversations, wonder about people's motivations, or reflect on how relationships develop and change.

Some individuals frequently imagine creative possibilities stories, designs, or ideas that could be built or expressed. Others repeatedly think about broader questions: how societies function, how technology evolves, or what shapes human behavior.

These recurring thoughts are rarely accidental.

Attention tends to return to subjects that carry personal meaning. Even when daily responsibilities demand focus elsewhere, the mind often revisits certain themes during quiet moments.

Consider what happens after finishing a long day of work.

Some people relax by reading about topics connected to their profession. Others explore subjects that have little connection to their job but reflect deeper curiosity psychology, science, philosophy, art, or emerging technologies.

The topics that consistently capture attention reveal something important.

They often point toward the kinds of problems a person naturally enjoys thinking about. These mental habits develop gradually and are shaped by both temperament and experience. Over time, they form a map of the mind's interests.

The difficulty is that many people rarely notice these patterns.

Modern environments encourage constant stimulation. Phones, notifications, and schedules fill the spaces where attention might otherwise wander freely. As a result, the quiet signals that appear in spontaneous thought can easily be overlooked.

Yet these signals are often reliable indicators of underlying priorities.

A person who repeatedly thinks about teaching others may care deeply about communication and learning. Someone who constantly analyzes systems may feel naturally drawn toward strategy or design. Another who often reflects on emotional dynamics may possess a strong interest in understanding human behavior.

None of these patterns immediately determine a career or life direction.

But they do reveal where attention naturally gravitates when it is not being directed by obligation.

One useful exercise is simply to observe these moments of wandering thought.

When your mind is free, where does it tend to go?

What kinds of questions appear again and again?

The answers to these questions may reveal topics that quietly occupy your mind more often than you realize.

13.2 Fascination Themes

If attention is observed across longer periods of time, another pattern often becomes visible: recurring fascination.

Most people can recall certain subjects that have captured their interest repeatedly throughout life. The specific form may change, but the underlying theme remains recognizable. A child fascinated by machines may later develop an interest in engineering, software, or complex systems. Someone drawn to stories and imagination early in life may eventually explore writing, filmmaking, or cultural analysis.

The fascination evolves, but the core curiosity persists.

These recurring interests are often easy to overlook because they develop gradually. At any single moment they may appear like ordinary hobbies or passing interests. Yet when viewed across several years or decades, they reveal surprising consistency.

For example, a person may notice that they have always been drawn toward understanding how systems work. As a child they might have taken apart objects to see how they functioned. Later they might analyze organizational structures, financial markets, or technological platforms with the same curiosity.

Another individual may realize that they have always been fascinated by human behavior. Early observations of friendships and social groups may later develop into interests in psychology, leadership, or cultural dynamics.

In many cases, fascination operates beneath the surface of formal responsibilities.

Someone working in a technical profession might spend their free time reading about philosophy or history. Another person employed in a structured corporate role may feel repeatedly drawn toward artistic expression or storytelling.

These patterns are rarely accidental.

Fascination usually emerges where intellectual or emotional engagement is strongest. It signals that the mind finds a particular type of question compelling. Even when circumstances change, the curiosity tends to reappear in new contexts.

This persistence suggests that fascination themes are connected to deeper aspects of identity.

They reflect how a person prefers to explore the world whether through analyzing systems, understanding people, creating ideas, building structures, or investigating complex questions.

Recognizing these themes requires looking backward as well as forward.

Which subjects have appeared repeatedly in your life? What kinds of ideas or problems have remained interesting even when circumstances changed?

When these questions are considered carefully, recurring fascinations often reveal patterns that were previously hidden in plain sight.

And those patterns may quietly point toward directions that feel naturally meaningful.

13.3 What You Research Without Obligation

Another revealing signal of attention appears in what people choose to learn when no one is asking them to.

Modern life provides access to an almost unlimited amount of information. Books, articles, podcasts, and online resources make it possible to explore nearly any subject within minutes. Yet despite this vast landscape of knowledge, most individuals repeatedly return to a relatively small set of topics.

What people research voluntarily often reveals more about their interests than what they study out of obligation.

In formal settings such as school or work, attention is directed by requirements. A student completes assignments because they are graded. A professional studies certain material because it is necessary for their role. These forms of learning can still be meaningful, but they are shaped by external expectations.

Curiosity-driven exploration behaves differently.

It appears when someone chooses to investigate a subject even though there is no clear reward for doing so. A person may spend hours reading about economic trends, psychological theories, design principles, technological innovations, historical events, or creative techniques simply because the topic feels interesting.

No deadline requires the effort. No supervisor demands the knowledge.

The motivation comes from within.

This form of voluntary learning often reveals authentic intellectual engagement. When curiosity is strong, the mind naturally seeks more information. Questions appear, and the individual follows them through articles, conversations, or personal experimentation.

Consider how people behave late at night when responsibilities are finished.

Some watch documentaries about science or history. Others explore discussions about entrepreneurship, philosophy, or cultural ideas. Someone else might spend hours studying visual design, music production, or new programming languages.

These patterns rarely emerge by accident.

When a person repeatedly returns to the same kinds of subjects during their free time, it suggests that the mind finds those questions inherently compelling.

Importantly, curiosity-driven exploration often appears long before it becomes part of a formal pursuit. A person may research a topic casually for years before realizing that the interest reflects a deeper fascination.

For this reason, voluntary learning can serve as a valuable indicator of authentic motivation.

It reveals the difference between what people feel they must know and what they genuinely want to understand.

One simple way to observe this signal is to notice what topics capture your attention when there is no external pressure.

When you open a book or search for information without any requirement to do so, what subjects do you explore?

The answers to that question often reveal where curiosity naturally leads.

13.4 Attention Logging Practice

Understanding attention requires more than occasional reflection. Because thoughts move quickly, the patterns that shape them can easily pass unnoticed. A subject may capture your interest repeatedly, yet if each moment is brief, the larger pattern remains invisible.

One practical way to make these patterns visible is through a simple exercise: attention logging.

The purpose of this practice is not to control your thoughts or force them in a particular direction. Instead, it is to observe where attention naturally goes during the course of ordinary life.

The method is straightforward.

During the day, take brief notes whenever you notice your attention returning to a particular topic or question. These observations do not need to be detailed. A short phrase is often enough:

- thinking about how technology platforms grow
- wondering why certain conversations feel engaging
- reading about behavioral psychology
- imagining ideas for a project or story

These notes capture small moments of curiosity or mental engagement. At first they may seem insignificant, but over time they accumulate.

After several days or weeks, patterns often begin to appear.

Certain themes show up repeatedly. The same kinds of questions return during quiet moments. Particular subjects appear across different contexts during conversations, reading, or casual browsing.

These recurring signals are valuable because they reveal attention as it actually behaves, rather than how we assume it behaves.

Many people believe they should care about certain topics because those subjects appear important within their profession or social environment. But attention logging often reveals a different reality. The mind repeatedly gravitates toward subjects that feel intellectually or emotionally engaging, regardless of external expectations.

The goal is not to immediately convert these interests into decisions about career or life direction.

Instead, the purpose is observation.

Over time, the log becomes a record of where your mind consistently invests its curiosity. These observations can highlight fascination themes, intellectual tendencies, and questions that carry deeper personal meaning.

A person who repeatedly records thoughts about human behavior may notice a strong interest in psychology or communication. Another who frequently returns to questions about systems, strategy, or technology may recognize an analytical fascination that appears across many situations.

Without deliberate observation, these signals often remain hidden in the background of daily activity.

With consistent observation, however, they begin to form a map.

And that map can offer something quietly valuable: evidence of where your attention naturally leads when it is free to wander.

Over time, learning to notice these patterns allows a person to recognize signals that might otherwise remain buried beneath routine obligations and distractions.

In this way, paying attention to your attention becomes a practical tool for discovering direction.

13.5 Attention Logging Practice

Recognizing patterns of attention is easier when those patterns are recorded over time.

Because thoughts appear and disappear quickly, it is difficult to notice recurring themes through memory alone. A subject may capture your interest several times during a week, but each moment may feel too small to remember clearly. Without some form of observation, these signals pass unnoticed.

One useful approach is a simple practice that can be called *attention logging.*

The goal is not to control your thoughts or analyze them immediately. Instead, the goal is simply to observe where attention naturally goes during ordinary moments of the day.

Whenever you notice your mind returning to a particular subject during a conversation, while reading, while browsing online, or during quiet moments write down a short note. The entry does not need to be detailed. A few words are enough.

For example, an entry might look like this:

- Thinking about how startups grow
- Curious about how people make career decisions
- Reading about behavioral psychology
- Imagining an idea for a system or product

These observations capture moments when attention becomes engaged without external obligation.

At first, the notes may appear scattered. But the practice becomes more valuable over time. After several days or ideally several weeks patterns often begin to emerge.

Certain subjects appear repeatedly.

You may notice that your mind returns frequently to questions about technology, human behavior, design, systems, storytelling, or social dynamics. Some topics generate repeated curiosity even when they are unrelated to your formal work or responsibilities.

These recurring themes are important because they reveal attention as it actually behaves.

Rather than asking abstract questions about what you *should* be interested in, the attention log shows what your mind consistently chooses to engage with.

Over time, the collection of observations begins to form a map of curiosity. It highlights subjects that generate intellectual energy and questions that the mind naturally enjoys exploring.

This map does not immediately determine what direction a person should pursue.

But it provides valuable information.

It shows where attention repeatedly returns, even when no reward or obligation requires it.

And when those patterns are observed consistently, they can reveal signals that point toward deeper interests and possible directions for growth.

Reflection Questions

1. What patterns appear in my attention?
2. Which activities increase my energy?
3. When did I last feel deeply engaged?

Chapter 14

Mapping Energy

Throughout the day, people experience subtle fluctuations in energy.

At certain moments the mind feels alert and engaged. Ideas come easily. Conversations feel stimulating. Work that might otherwise seem demanding becomes absorbing. At other times, even simple tasks feel heavy. Attention drifts, motivation fades, and effort requires deliberate discipline.

Many individuals assume these changes are simply random variations in mood or fatigue.

But when observed over longer periods, patterns often begin to appear.

Certain kinds of activities consistently produce a sense of vitality. Particular environments make thinking clearer or more creative. Some conversations generate excitement, while others create quiet exhaustion.

These variations are rarely accidental.

Energy often reflects the degree of alignment between a person and the situation they are in. When the nature of a task, environment, or interaction fits the way someone naturally thinks and engages with the world, vitality tends to increase. When the fit is weaker, energy gradually declines.

Observing these patterns can therefore reveal valuable information.

Instead of relying only on abstract ideas about what someone *should* enjoy or succeed at, energy provides a more immediate signal. It shows how the body and mind actually respond to different activities and environments.

Learning to notice these responses and to map them over time can reveal where a person naturally feels engaged, capable, and alive.

14.1 Vitality Moments

Most people can recall moments when their energy suddenly rises.

A conversation becomes stimulating and ideas begin to flow easily. A difficult problem captures attention so completely that distractions fade away. A project that once seemed ordinary becomes absorbing as new possibilities appear.

During these moments, effort feels different.

The mind becomes sharper. Concentration strengthens. Instead of pushing through tasks with discipline alone, a person feels naturally drawn into the activity. Time may pass quickly without being noticed.

These experiences are often described as moments of vitality.

Vitality does not necessarily mean excitement in the dramatic sense. It is usually quieter than that. It appears as a sense of mental clarity, engagement, and interest. The individual feels awake to what they are doing.

These moments can occur in many different situations.

A teacher may feel energized while explaining an idea to others. A strategist may experience vitality when analyzing a complex system. A writer may feel most alive when shaping language to express a thought clearly. Someone fascinated by human behavior may find conversations about relationships or motivations deeply engaging.

In each case, the activity resonates with the person's natural tendencies.

Vitality often appears where curiosity, ability, and environment align. The task matches the way the person prefers to think or interact with the world. Instead of forcing attention, the activity invites it.

This is why moments of vitality are such useful signals.

They reveal not only what someone is capable of doing, but what kinds of activities naturally activate their attention and energy. While discipline and persistence are important in any field, sustained engagement is easier when the underlying activity produces vitality rather than resistance.

Unfortunately, many people overlook these signals.

Daily routines often focus on responsibilities rather than engagement. Tasks are completed because they are required, not because they generate energy. As a result, moments of vitality may appear briefly but go unnoticed.

Yet when these moments are observed carefully, patterns begin to appear.

Certain types of problems repeatedly generate interest. Particular kinds of conversations stimulate thinking. Some environments make learning feel effortless while others create quiet fatigue.

These patterns are not accidental.

They reflect the areas where a person's natural strengths and interests intersect with their activities. Over time, these signals can provide valuable clues about where deeper alignment may exist.

A useful starting point is simply to notice when these moments occur.

During what kinds of activities do you feel mentally energized?

What conversations, problems, or forms of work seem to wake up your attention rather than drain it?

Reflecting on these questions can begin to reveal the situations in which your energy naturally rises.

14.2 Flow States

Beyond brief moments of vitality, there are deeper forms of engagement in which attention becomes fully absorbed in an activity. These experiences are often described as *flow states.*

The concept was introduced by psychologist *Mihaly Csikszentmihalyi*, who observed that people sometimes enter a state of deep concentration in which the mind becomes completely engaged with a task.

During flow, attention narrows naturally and distractions fade into the background. A person becomes immersed in what they are doing, sometimes to the point where their awareness of time shifts. Minutes pass quickly, or entire hours disappear without being noticed.

The experience is familiar to many people.

A writer may begin working on a paragraph and suddenly realize that an entire afternoon has passed. A programmer may become absorbed in solving a technical problem, focusing so deeply that interruptions feel unusually disruptive. A musician may practice for hours while feeling that only a short period has gone by.

In each case, the activity holds attention completely.

Psychological research suggests that flow tends to appear when two conditions are balanced: challenge and skill. The task must be demanding enough to require concentration, yet not so difficult that it becomes overwhelming. When the level of challenge matches a person's abilities, the mind becomes naturally engaged.

This balance produces a distinctive mental state.

The activity feels meaningful in itself. Effort is still required, but it no longer feels forced. Instead of pushing through resistance, the person becomes absorbed in the process of solving, creating, or understanding.

For this reason, flow experiences often feel intrinsically rewarding.

The satisfaction does not come primarily from external outcomes such as recognition or completion. It emerges from the experience of doing the activity itself. The mind finds the process engaging enough that the activity becomes its own reward.

Over time, repeated experiences of flow can reveal important patterns.

A person might notice that deep immersion appears most often while explaining ideas, analyzing systems, designing solutions, or exploring creative expression. Another individual might consistently experience flow when building things, conducting research, or engaging in strategic thinking.

These recurring experiences are significant because they show where attention naturally sustains itself.

Not every meaningful activity produces flow, and not every flow experience must determine a career or life direction. But when a person repeatedly enters this state during certain kinds of tasks, it often suggests that the activity aligns well with their cognitive style and interests.

Noticing moments of flow can therefore provide valuable information.

They reveal where concentration becomes effortless, where curiosity remains active, and where engagement feels deeply natural.

By observing when and where these states occur, individuals can begin identifying the kinds of work or activities that may represent meaningful directions.

14.3 Environmental Effects

Energy does not arise only from the tasks a person performs. It is also shaped by the environments in which those tasks occur.

Physical surroundings influence attention in subtle but powerful ways. Some people find their concentration strongest in quiet spaces where interruptions are minimal. Others think more clearly in environments filled with activity and conversation. A writer may work best in solitude, while an entrepreneur may feel energized in rooms where ideas move quickly between people.

Lighting, noise, structure, and even the arrangement of space can affect mental clarity. A cluttered desk may create distraction for one person while leaving another unaffected. A structured office environment may support focus for some individuals but feel restrictive to others who prefer more flexible settings.

These environmental differences often remain unnoticed because people assume that productivity should look the same for everyone.

In reality, individuals respond differently to their surroundings.

Social environments play a similar role. Some people feel energized when collaborating with others, exchanging ideas and building momentum through conversation. Others perform best when they have time to think independently before sharing their conclusions.

Confidence and engagement often shift depending on the people present.

A person may feel comfortable expressing ideas within a small, thoughtful group but become quiet in large competitive environments. Another may thrive in fast-moving discussions but struggle when work requires extended solitary concentration.

In these situations, the difference is not necessarily a matter of ability.

Instead, the environment may be amplifying or suppressing particular strengths.

Consider someone whose thinking style is analytical and reflective. In a workplace that rewards quick responses and constant verbal participation, their strengths may remain underused. Yet in a setting that allows deeper analysis and careful problem-solving, the same person may perform exceptionally well.

Another individual might possess strong interpersonal instincts that flourish in collaborative settings but remain hidden in isolated environments.

Recognizing these patterns can shift how people interpret their experiences.

What appears to be a personal limitation may sometimes be an environmental mismatch. When the setting does not support a person's natural way of working or thinking, energy gradually declines. When the environment aligns with those tendencies, energy often increases.

For this reason, observing environmental effects can reveal where someone is most likely to thrive.

Which settings make concentration easier? Where do conversations feel energizing rather than exhausting? In what environments do your strengths become more visible?

These questions highlight the relationship between personal energy and context.

Understanding that relationship allows individuals to design conditions that support their engagement more effectively. By choosing environments that align with their natural tendencies, they can create contexts where their abilities and energy have greater room to develop.

14.4 Patterns Across Contexts

Individual moments of vitality or fatigue can be informative, but the most useful insights often appear when energy is observed across many situations.

A single experience may reflect temporary circumstances. An engaging conversation might feel energizing simply because it was new or unexpected. A difficult task might feel draining because it occurred during a stressful week. Taken alone, these moments can be misleading.

Patterns become clearer when experiences are compared across different contexts.

Consider how your energy behaves in several areas of life: during work, while learning new subjects, in conversations with others, or when pursuing personal projects. Each of these environments offers opportunities to notice how attention and motivation respond.

Some situations repeatedly generate engagement.

A person might notice that discussions about ideas consistently bring energy, whether those conversations occur in a classroom, a workplace meeting, or an informal discussion with friends. Another individual may find that solving complex problems feels stimulating across many settings during professional work, while learning new skills, or even while playing strategic games.

Other situations show the opposite pattern.

Certain environments may consistently produce fatigue. Meetings focused on routine details might feel draining regardless of the organization involved. Tasks requiring constant social interaction may exhaust someone who prefers extended periods of independent thinking.

When these responses repeat across different environments, they begin to reveal something important.

The pattern suggests that the energy response is not caused by a single circumstance. Instead, it reflects a deeper relationship between the person's cognitive style, interests, and the nature of the activity.

For example, someone who consistently feels energized by teaching, mentoring, or explaining ideas may possess a natural inclination toward communication and learning. Another person who repeatedly experiences engagement while designing systems or solving technical problems may be drawn toward analytical or structural thinking.

Recognizing these patterns requires observing experiences across time and context.

Ask yourself: in what kinds of situations does my energy consistently rise? Where does it reliably decline? Which activities feel sustainable across different environments?

The answers often reveal signals that are difficult to see when each experience is considered separately.

When energy patterns remain consistent across many situations, they point toward environments and activities where a person is most likely to thrive.

And over time, those consistent signals often reveal something deeper: the kinds of contexts in which a person naturally belongs.

Reflection Questions

1. What patterns appear in my attention?
2. Which activities increase my energy?
3. When did I last feel deeply engaged?

Chapter 15

Experimentation

After observing signals patterns of attention, fluctuations in energy, and emotional responses a natural question appears:

What should I do with this information?

For many people, the instinct is to search for a clear decision. They try to determine the correct career, the right project, or the single direction that will resolve their uncertainty. Because the choice feels significant, the decision begins to feel heavy, as if it must determine the future all at once.

But life rarely unfolds through one decisive choice.

More often, direction emerges gradually through experience. Interests become clearer as people try different activities. Skills develop through repeated practice. What once felt uncertain begins to make sense after direct engagement with the work itself.

In this sense, discovering direction resembles a process of experimentation.

Instead of treating uncertainty as a problem that must be solved before action begins, experimentation treats uncertainty as information that can only be understood through action.

The goal is not to find a perfect answer immediately.

The goal is to learn.

15.1 Small Tests Instead of Big Decisions

One of the reasons people feel stuck when thinking about direction is that the decisions appear too large.

Questions about careers, life paths, or major changes often arrive in the form of a single, overwhelming choice. Should I change fields? Should I pursue this interest seriously? Should I leave what I am doing now and begin something new?

When framed this way, the decision carries enormous weight. It appears to determine years of future effort, financial stability, reputation, and personal identity. Because the stakes feel so high, hesitation becomes natural. People wait for certainty before acting.

But certainty rarely appears in advance.

Many forms of meaningful work cannot be fully understood until they are experienced directly. The daily rhythm of the work, the type of problems involved, and the environment surrounding it often reveal themselves only through participation.

For this reason, large life decisions are often easier to approach through smaller experiments.

Instead of asking whether a new direction should become a permanent commitment, a person can begin by asking a simpler question: what would it look like to test this interest on a small scale?

A small test might involve dedicating a few hours each week to exploring a new skill. It might mean volunteering in an environment related to a field of interest, starting a small personal project, or collaborating with someone already working in that area.

These experiments are limited in scope.

Because they are temporary and manageable, they remove much of the pressure associated with a major decision. The individual is not committing to a permanent identity or abandoning their current path. They are simply gathering information.

This shift in perspective changes how exploration feels.

Instead of asking, "What if this choice turns out to be wrong?" the person begins asking, "What can I learn from trying this?"

Short-term experiments often reveal insights that speculation alone cannot provide. A person might discover that an activity they imagined enjoying actually feels tedious in practice. Another might find that a small project generates unexpected excitement and engagement.

In both cases, the experiment provides valuable information.

Small tests also make exploration reversible. If the activity does not resonate, the person can step away with minimal disruption. If the interest deepens, the experiment can gradually expand.

Over time, these small explorations accumulate into a clearer understanding of what fits.

Rather than demanding immediate certainty about the future, experimentation allows direction to emerge gradually.

A few hours of exploration, repeated over weeks or months, can reveal far more about a path than long periods of speculation.

And in many cases, these small experiments provide exactly what people need most when facing uncertainty: insight without requiring long-term commitment.

15.2 Trying Identities Temporarily

Many people hesitate to explore new directions because they believe identity must change all at once.

If someone has spent years being known as a lawyer, engineer, manager, or researcher, considering another role may feel like a dramatic shift. The change appears absolute, as though one identity must be abandoned before another can begin.

This belief makes exploration difficult.

In reality, identities rarely change in a single step. More often, they evolve gradually through experience. Before someone fully adopts a new role, they usually spend time experimenting with it in smaller ways.

Temporary exploration allows a person to step into a possible identity without making a permanent commitment.

For example, someone curious about teaching might begin by mentoring younger colleagues or leading workshops. A professional interested in writing might start publishing essays or maintaining a small online journal. Someone drawn toward entrepreneurship might test ideas through small projects while maintaining their current work.

These activities create opportunities to experience the role directly.

Instead of imagining what it might feel like to be a teacher, writer, or founder, the individual begins performing some of the activities associated with that identity. Through practice, they observe how the role actually feels.

Does the work generate curiosity and energy? Do the challenges feel engaging or discouraging? Does the activity bring out strengths that were previously unnoticed?

Temporary exploration often reveals unexpected insights.

A person who believed they lacked creative ability may discover that they enjoy designing or writing when given the chance to experiment. Another who imagined a certain role as exciting may realize that its daily responsibilities do not match their preferences.

Both discoveries are valuable.

By trying identities in small ways, individuals gather information about how those roles align with their interests, abilities, and values. The experiment turns abstract ideas into lived experience.

Importantly, this approach also reduces the fear of making a wrong decision.

When identity is treated as something that must be chosen permanently, uncertainty feels threatening. But when identity is approached as something that can be explored gradually, uncertainty becomes easier to tolerate.

The person is not committing to a fixed label.

They are simply learning what different roles feel like in practice.

Over time, these experiments begin to shape identity in subtle ways. Activities that feel meaningful receive more attention, while others gradually fade. Interests deepen in some areas and lose energy in others.

Through this process, identity becomes less about choosing a single definition and more about discovering what naturally fits.

Rather than requiring immediate certainty, identity can develop through exploration.

15.3 Learning From Action

Reflection plays an important role in understanding direction. Thinking carefully about interests, values, and patterns of attention can reveal useful signals. Yet reflection alone has limits.

Ideas formed in the mind are often incomplete.

When people imagine a possible path, they tend to focus on the aspects that are easiest to picture. A profession may appear appealing because of its reputation, the lifestyle associated with it, or the kinds of problems it seems to involve. But imagination rarely captures the full experience of the work.

Only action reveals how something actually feels in practice.

When a person begins doing the work itself writing, teaching, designing, building, researching, managing, or creating the experience becomes concrete. The rhythm of the activity becomes clearer. The kinds of challenges involved become visible. Strengths and weaknesses begin to emerge.

A task that looked exciting from a distance may feel tedious when repeated daily. Another activity that seemed ordinary may become unexpectedly engaging once someone begins working with it directly.

Action therefore produces feedback that speculation cannot provide.

Through experience, people begin to see how their abilities interact with real situations. They notice where their thinking feels sharp and where it struggles. They learn which kinds of problems sustain their attention and which gradually drain their energy.

Even mistakes become valuable in this process.

When an experiment does not work as expected, it often reveals something important. A failed project may show that a certain type of work does not match a person's interests. An unexpected difficulty may highlight skills that need development. A surprising success may reveal abilities that were previously overlooked.

In this way, action becomes a powerful form of learning.

Each attempt produces information. The results refine understanding of what fits and what does not. Over time, these experiences accumulate into a clearer sense of direction.

This process also changes how uncertainty is experienced.

Instead of remaining an abstract question—*Would this path be right for me?* uncertainty becomes something that can be explored through direct engagement.

By acting, observing the results, and adjusting accordingly, individuals gradually transform uncertainty into information.

15.4 Iteration as Growth

Rarely does a single experiment provide a complete answer about direction.

More often, understanding develops through a series of small adjustments.

A person tries an activity, observes what happens, and then modifies their approach. Each step provides a little more information about what feels engaging, what feels difficult, and what seems worth exploring further.

This process resembles iteration.

In many fields science, engineering, design, or entrepreneurship progress rarely appears in a single breakthrough. Instead, improvement occurs through cycles of testing and refinement. An idea is tried, the results are observed, and the next attempt becomes slightly more informed than the last.

Personal direction often develops in the same way.

One experiment may reveal that a particular activity sparks curiosity but requires different skills than expected. Another attempt may show that certain environments increase motivation while others create resistance. A project that begins as a simple exploration may evolve into something more substantial once its potential becomes clearer.

Each experience adds a piece of information.

Over time, these pieces begin to form a clearer picture of where attention, energy, and ability intersect. The person does not need to predict the final destination at the beginning. Instead, direction gradually becomes visible through repeated interaction with the world.

Iteration also changes how confidence develops.

When people believe they must make a perfect decision immediately, hesitation increases. The fear of choosing incorrectly becomes overwhelming. But when direction is approached as an evolving process, each small experiment becomes an opportunity to learn rather than a test that must be passed.

With every iteration, uncertainty becomes easier to navigate.

A person begins to trust that adjustments are possible. If one approach does not fit, another can be tried. Gradually, the path becomes more refined as experience accumulates.

Seen this way, personal growth is less like choosing a single road and more like navigating through a landscape.

The route becomes clearer not through one decisive moment, but through many small steps taken with attention and curiosity.

And in many lives, direction does not emerge from a single defining decision.

It emerges through a series of thoughtful adjustments, each one guided by what has been learned along the way.

Reflection Questions

1. What patterns appear in my attention?
2. Which activities increase my energy?
3. When did I last feel deeply engaged?

Chapter 16

Constructing Your Narrative

Throughout this book we have explored different kinds of signals patterns of attention, fluctuations in energy, emotional responses, curiosity, and the results of experimentation. Each of these signals offers a small piece of information about who a person is and how they engage with the world.

Yet these signals rarely exist in isolation.

They accumulate gradually across years of experience. Interests appear, fade, and sometimes return in new forms. Skills develop slowly through practice. Encounters with different people and environments reshape how someone understands themselves.

When viewed moment by moment, these experiences can seem scattered. Life appears to unfold through a series of unrelated events education, work, relationships, opportunities, and mistakes.

But when these experiences are examined together, patterns often begin to emerge.

The human mind naturally organizes experience through narrative. We understand our lives not only as individual memories but as stories that connect those memories across time. Through narrative, events that once seemed separate begin to reveal relationships with one another.

Earlier experiences influence later decisions. Interests that appeared briefly in one stage may reappear in another. What once looked like coincidence may reveal a deeper continuity.

Constructing a personal narrative therefore becomes a powerful way to observe identity.

By examining how different moments connect across time, people can begin to see the underlying themes that have quietly guided their attention, decisions, and development.

16.1 Connecting Experiences

When people look back on their lives, they often remember events as isolated moments.

School years are remembered separately from early work experiences. A career change may appear disconnected from childhood interests. Relationships, projects, successes, and failures may each occupy their own place in memory, like separate chapters without an obvious link between them.

Seen this way, life can appear fragmented.

A person might describe their past as a series of unrelated choices: the subject they studied, the job they accepted, the opportunities they pursued or declined. Each event seems shaped by circumstances at the time rather than by any deeper pattern.

Yet when these experiences are examined more carefully, connections often begin to appear.

The interest that guided a career decision may have first appeared years earlier in a different form. A skill developed in one environment may later become valuable in another. Even decisions that seemed accidental at the time may reveal a consistent motivation when viewed in hindsight.

Consider someone who spent childhood fascinated by organizing events among friends. At the time, this interest might have seemed like simple social enthusiasm. Later, however, the same person might find themselves drawn toward roles involving coordination, leadership, or community-building.

What once appeared as separate activities begins to reveal a common thread.

Another person may recall spending long hours trying to understand how things work taking apart devices, experimenting with software, or asking questions about systems and structures. Years later, they might find themselves naturally drawn toward engineering, strategy, or analytical problem-solving.

In these examples, early experiences do not determine the future.

But they often contain signals that reappear in different contexts.

Connecting experiences allows these signals to become visible.

Instead of viewing life as a sequence of disconnected events, individuals begin to see how certain motivations, curiosities, or patterns of thinking persist across time. Turning points that once seemed random begin to make more sense when placed within a broader story.

Reflection plays an important role in this process.

When people step back and examine how their experiences relate to one another, they often discover that their past contains more coherence than they originally believed. Choices that once felt uncertain may reveal underlying patterns of interest or value.

These connections do not produce a single predetermined path.

But they can clarify the direction that has quietly shaped many earlier decisions.

One way to begin this reflection is by asking a simple question:

Which experiences in your life seem to share a common thread?

Looking for connections between moments that once appeared separate can reveal patterns that were present all along.

16.2 Identifying Themes

Once experiences begin to connect, another layer of understanding often appears: recurring themes.

A theme is a pattern that appears repeatedly across different stages of life. The context may change, but the underlying interest, value, or motivation remains similar. When people reflect carefully on their experiences, these themes often become surprisingly visible.

At first, they may seem subtle.

An individual might notice that they have repeatedly been drawn toward explaining ideas to others. In school, they helped classmates understand difficult concepts. Later, they mentored colleagues or found satisfaction in teaching or writing about complex topics.

The environments may differ, but the theme remains the same.

Another person might recognize a long-standing fascination with systems how organizations function, how technologies interact, or how complex problems can be broken down into smaller parts. This curiosity may appear in different forms over time, yet the intellectual orientation remains consistent.

Themes also appear through values.

Some individuals repeatedly choose paths that emphasize stability and responsibility. Others consistently gravitate toward exploration and innovation. Some prioritize collaboration and community, while others prefer independent work and deep concentration.

These preferences shape decisions even when the person is not consciously aware of them.

Patterns may also appear in relationships and learning. A person might notice that they are often the one who helps resolve conflicts or clarify misunderstandings. Another may realize they are consistently drawn toward learning new skills and exploring unfamiliar ideas.

When these observations are placed side by side, they begin to reveal a deeper structure.

Identity is not formed only by isolated decisions. It develops through recurring orientations toward certain kinds of experiences. The mind returns to similar questions, values shape similar choices, and certain environments repeatedly attract attention.

Recognizing these themes can be illuminating.

Instead of asking what direction should come next in an abstract sense, individuals can examine what has already appeared repeatedly in their lives. The themes reveal what has quietly mattered over time.

Looking back, you might ask yourself:

What interests have appeared again and again in different forms?

What values have influenced my decisions across different stages of life?

Answering these questions often reveals that certain elements have been present far longer than expected.

And recognizing those themes can provide valuable insight into what consistently matters to you.

16.3 Discovering Meaning in Story

Human beings naturally understand their lives through stories.

When people describe who they are, they rarely list isolated facts. Instead, they recount events moments of decision, periods of struggle, unexpected opportunities, turning points that shaped later choices. These events become meaningful not simply because they occurred, but because they are woven together into a narrative.

Narrative provides coherence.

Without it, experiences can feel scattered and confusing. A failed project may appear as nothing more than a mistake. A career change may seem like evidence of uncertainty. Difficult periods may feel disconnected from later successes.

But when these experiences are placed within a broader story, their meaning often changes.

A failed project might reveal the beginning of an important lesson. A career change may become a transition that introduced new interests or abilities. A difficult period may appear, in retrospect, as the moment that redirected attention toward something more meaningful.

The events themselves do not change.

What changes is the interpretation.

Narrative allows individuals to see how earlier experiences contributed to later development. A challenge that once seemed like a setback may later appear as preparation. A seemingly accidental opportunity may reveal itself as a turning point that shaped the direction of many future decisions.

Consider someone who spent years in a career that eventually felt misaligned.

At the time, those years may have seemed like a detour. Yet when the experience is placed within a narrative, it may reveal valuable skills that later became essential in a different field. The person did not simply change direction they carried insights and abilities from one stage of the story into the next.

This perspective transforms how change is understood.

Instead of viewing life as a sequence of unrelated choices, narrative allows individuals to see continuity within change. Growth becomes easier to recognize because each stage contributes to the unfolding story.

Narrative also provides a sense of orientation.

When people reflect on their past through the lens of story, they often begin to see how their present interests emerged from earlier experiences. Curiosity that appears today may have been developing quietly for years. Values that guide current decisions may have been shaped by moments that once seemed minor.

Through storytelling, confusion gradually becomes more understandable.

Patterns appear where randomness once seemed to dominate. The individual begins to see themselves not simply as someone reacting to circumstances, but as a person whose experiences form part of a developing narrative.

Meaning often emerges through this process.

It becomes visible when events are not viewed as isolated moments, but as connected elements of a larger story.

16.4 Writing Your Personal Biography

Understanding the narrative of a life becomes easier when it is written down.

Most people carry fragments of their past in memory important moments, decisions, successes, and disappointments. Yet these memories often remain scattered. They exist as individual recollections rather than as parts of a coherent story.

Writing a brief personal biography can help bring these fragments together.

The purpose of this exercise is not to produce a detailed autobiography. Instead, it is a reflective practice designed to help you observe the structure of your own experiences. By describing the major stages of your life in a few pages, patterns that once felt invisible often begin to appear.

You might begin by identifying several important periods.

These could include early interests during childhood, educational choices, formative relationships, career decisions, projects that mattered to you, or moments when your perspective changed significantly. Rather than listing events chronologically, focus on the experiences that felt influential.

As you write, ask yourself simple questions.

Which moments seemed to redirect your path? What decisions felt especially meaningful at the time? Which experiences shaped how you understand yourself today?

Often a few turning points stand out.

Perhaps a mentor introduced an idea that changed how you think. A challenge forced you to develop new abilities. An opportunity revealed interests that had previously been unnoticed.

Once these moments are written down, another step becomes possible:

looking for patterns.

Do certain interests appear repeatedly across different stages of life? Do particular values seem to guide many of your decisions? Have you often been drawn toward similar types of problems, environments, or relationships?

Sometimes the same motivations appear in different forms. A person who enjoyed explaining ideas to classmates may later find satisfaction in mentoring colleagues or teaching. Someone fascinated by systems as a child may eventually pursue work that involves strategy, design, or analysis.

By observing these patterns, the narrative of your life becomes clearer.

Experiences that once seemed unrelated begin to connect. Choices that felt uncertain at the time may reveal a consistent direction when viewed across many years.

Importantly, this narrative is not fixed.

As new experiences accumulate, the story continues to evolve. Interests deepen, values shift, and unexpected opportunities introduce new chapters. For this reason, it can be valuable to revisit your personal biography periodically.

Each time you reflect on your story, new patterns may become visible.

And over time, this ongoing narrative can help reveal the deeper signals that continue to shape your identity and direction.

Part V

LIVING FROM ALIGNMENT

Chapter 17

Acting Without Certainty

Many people delay important decisions because they are waiting for clarity.

They hope that one day the right direction will become obvious. A moment of certainty will appear, removing doubt and making the next step clear. Once that clarity arrives, action will feel safe.

But life rarely provides certainty in advance.

Most meaningful paths reveal themselves only after movement begins. Interests deepen through practice. Skills become visible through use. Environments that once seemed appealing reveal their true character only when experienced directly.

Waiting for complete certainty therefore creates a paradox.

The clarity people are waiting for often appears only after they begin acting.

This does not mean decisions should be made impulsively or without reflection. Thoughtful observation of signals patterns of attention, shifts in energy, curiosity, and emotional responses can provide valuable guidance. Yet reflection alone cannot produce the full picture.

Action adds information.

By moving forward, even in small ways, individuals begin to see how their expectations interact with reality. Experiences provide feedback that speculation cannot. Gradually, through interaction with the world, direction becomes clearer.

17.1 Movement Creates Clarity

Many people believe that clarity must come before action.

They assume that the correct path should first become visible in thought, and only then should effort begin. Decisions about careers, projects, or personal direction are therefore postponed until the mind feels certain.

This approach feels rational.

After all, careful thinking can prevent unnecessary mistakes. Reflection allows individuals to consider alternatives, examine their motivations, and anticipate possible consequences. In complex situations, thoughtful analysis is valuable.

Yet reflection alone has limits.

When people try to imagine a path without participating in it, the mind relies on incomplete information. Assumptions fill the gaps. The imagined experience may emphasize the appealing aspects while overlooking the routine challenges that accompany the work.

A profession may seem exciting because of its visible achievements, but the daily activities involved remain abstract. A project may appear manageable in theory, yet the practical difficulties only become clear once the work begins.

Action changes this.

When a person takes even a small step into a new activity, they begin receiving direct feedback. The experience reveals details that were invisible during reflection. Certain aspects of the work may feel engaging, while others feel draining. Skills that seemed uncertain may begin to develop through practice.

Consider someone curious about writing.

They might spend months thinking about whether they have the ability or discipline required. But the moment they begin writing regularly, the question becomes easier to evaluate. The act itself reveals whether the process generates energy or resistance.

The same pattern appears in many areas of life.

A person wondering whether they would enjoy teaching learns far more by mentoring someone than by imagining the role from a distance. Someone interested in starting a business gains insight by testing a small idea rather than analyzing possibilities indefinitely.

In each case, movement produces information.

Small steps are often enough to begin this process. A short project, a volunteer experience, or a brief collaboration can reveal how a particular direction feels in practice. These experiments rarely answer every question, but they transform uncertainty into experience.

Over time, the accumulation of these experiences gradually clarifies direction.

Instead of relying only on speculation, individuals begin learning from participation. They see how their attention, energy, and abilities respond in real situations.

Clarity, in this sense, is not something that appears before action.

More often, it emerges through the act of engaging with the world itself.

17.2 Iterative Decision-Making

One reason decisions feel so heavy is the assumption that they must be correct the first time.

When people think about choosing a direction whether in work, study, or personal projects they often imagine the decision as permanent. A single choice appears capable of determining years of future effort. If the decision is wrong, the consequences seem difficult to reverse.

This way of thinking creates unnecessary pressure.

In reality, many decisions are not final commitments. They are starting points.

Paths evolve as new information becomes available. Projects change shape once they begin. Interests deepen in some areas while fading in others. Most meaningful work develops through a series of adjustments rather than through a perfectly chosen initial step.

This process is often described as iterative decision-making.

Instead of trying to predict the entire path in advance, a person makes a reasonable decision based on the information currently available. They observe the results, learn from the experience, and then adjust their next step accordingly.

Many fields operate this way.

Engineers test prototypes and refine their designs through repeated experiments. Entrepreneurs launch small versions of ideas and adapt based on feedback from the real world. Researchers revise their hypotheses as new evidence appears.

The same principle can apply to personal direction.

A person might begin exploring a new skill, join a collaborative project, or take on a role that seems promising. As the experience unfolds, they observe how their attention, energy, and abilities respond. Some aspects of the work may feel engaging, while others reveal limitations or unexpected challenges.

These observations become valuable information.

Instead of seeing early outcomes as proof of success or failure, they can be treated as feedback. The individual learns something about how the activity fits with their interests and capacities. That insight then informs the next adjustment.

This perspective reduces the pressure to make perfect choices.

When decisions are understood as part of an evolving process, the first step does not need to solve everything. It simply needs to move the person forward enough to reveal new information.

Over time, this cycle of action and adjustment gradually clarifies direction.

What begins as a tentative exploration may develop into a sustained interest. A path that initially seemed promising may reveal its limitations, allowing the person to redirect their effort toward something more aligned.

Seen in this way, decisions are less like final judgments and more like ongoing conversations with experience.

Each step invites a response, and each response helps shape the next step.

Approaching decisions as iterative processes allows direction to emerge gradually rather than demanding immediate certainty.

17.3 Trusting Direction Over Guarantees

One of the most common reasons people hesitate to act is the desire for guarantees.

Before committing to a decision, many individuals hope for reassurance that the outcome will be successful. They want evidence that the effort will be worthwhile, that the risks will remain manageable, and that the path they choose will lead to a stable future.

This desire for certainty is understandable.

Important choices often involve time, reputation, financial stability, and personal identity. When the consequences feel significant, the mind naturally searches for reassurance before moving forward.

Yet meaningful decisions rarely come with guarantees.

The environments in which people live and work are constantly changing. Industries evolve, technologies shift, and opportunities appear in unexpected ways. Even paths that seem stable can transform over time.

Because of this uncertainty, waiting for perfect assurance can lead to prolonged hesitation.

Instead of external guarantees, what people often possess is something quieter: a sense of internal direction.

This direction does not appear as complete certainty about the future. Rather, it emerges through the signals explored throughout this book curiosity about certain questions, energy that appears during particular activities, fascination with specific problems, or values that consistently influence decisions.

These signals do not promise outcomes.

But they provide orientation.

For example, someone may not know whether pursuing a creative project will lead to recognition or financial stability. Yet the repeated experience of engagement while working on the project may signal that the activity aligns with how they think and create.

Another person may not know whether exploring a new field will produce long-term success. But their sustained curiosity about the subject suggests that the exploration itself may be meaningful.

Over time, confidence develops through interaction with these signals.

Each step taken in alignment with curiosity or engagement produces new experiences. Some experiments succeed, others fail, but both contribute to learning. Gradually the individual becomes more familiar with their own patterns of interest and energy.

This familiarity builds trust.

Instead of relying entirely on external validation, people begin recognizing that their internal responses can guide decisions in situations where certainty is unavailable.

Trusting direction does not eliminate uncertainty.

It simply acknowledges that uncertainty is part of most meaningful pursuits.

When individuals learn to act despite that uncertainty guided by their signals rather than by guarantees they often discover that clarity and confidence grow through experience.

In this sense, trusting direction requires accepting that some uncertainty will always remain.

17.4 Leaving the Myth of Perfect Choices

A powerful source of hesitation is the belief that somewhere there exists a single perfect decision.

People often imagine that among all possible careers, projects, or life paths there must be one option that is clearly correct. If they could only identify that choice in advance, everything would fall into place. Success would follow naturally, and the uncertainty that surrounds decision-making would disappear.

This belief is understandable, but it creates unnecessary pressure.

When someone assumes that only one path is correct, every decision begins to feel like a high-stakes test. The mind searches for certainty that cannot realistically be obtained. Each possibility is examined repeatedly, yet none appears flawless enough to justify commitment.

The result is often overthinking.

Instead of moving forward, individuals remain suspended in analysis. They compare options endlessly, searching for the perfect alignment of opportunity, security, and meaning. The fear of making a mistake grows stronger than the desire to explore.

Yet the structure of real life rarely supports the idea of a single correct choice.

Many paths can lead to growth. Different environments can cultivate different abilities. Experiences that begin in one field may later translate into opportunities in another. Skills developed along one route often become valuable in ways that were impossible to predict beforehand.

What appears to be a "wrong" decision may later reveal itself as a necessary stage of development.

A job that seemed temporary may teach skills that later become essential. A project that does not succeed may clarify what kind of work actually feels meaningful. Even detours often contribute knowledge that shapes future direction.

When this perspective becomes clearer, the myth of perfect choices begins to lose its power.

Instead of searching for an ideal path that guarantees success, individuals can approach decisions as starting points. Each choice opens a particular set of experiences, relationships, and learning opportunities. From there, the path continues to evolve.

Releasing the expectation of perfection creates psychological freedom.

It allows people to choose a direction based on the best information currently available rather than waiting for complete certainty. The decision becomes less about selecting the flawless option and more about beginning a process of exploration.

Progress rarely comes from identifying a perfect path in advance.

More often, it emerges when someone chooses a direction, learns from the experience, and adapts along the way.

Chapter 18

Designing an Aligned Life

Understanding oneself is only the beginning of the process.

Throughout this book we have explored different kinds of signals patterns of attention, fluctuations in energy, recurring fascinations, emotional responses, and the lessons revealed through experimentation. Together, these signals help people understand how they naturally think, what they value, and where their curiosity tends to lead.

But insight alone does not change a life.

Self-understanding becomes meaningful when it begins to shape the structures through which a person lives. Work, relationships, environments, and daily routines all influence how identity is expressed. When these structures align with a person's internal patterns, life often feels more coherent and sustainable. When they conflict with those patterns, even success can feel strangely disconnected.

Designing an aligned life therefore involves translating insight into practical choices.

This process rarely requires dramatic transformation. More often, it unfolds through gradual adjustments small changes in responsibilities, environments, relationships, or schedules that bring everyday life closer to one's internal direction.

Alignment is not a single decision.

It is an ongoing process of shaping the conditions in which a person lives and works so that their external life reflects their internal signals more clearly.

18.1 Work Alignment

For many adults, work occupies a significant portion of daily life.

Because of this, the relationship between work and personal patterns has a powerful influence on how life feels overall. When the activities that fill a workday align with a person's natural interests and ways of thinking, effort often feels purposeful and engaging. When the alignment is weak, even successful careers can feel strangely exhausting.

Work alignment does not necessarily mean finding a completely different profession.

Often the difference lies in how a role emphasizes certain skills or tendencies. Within the same field, individuals may engage with very different aspects of the work. One person may thrive in analytical problem-solving, another in communication and teaching, and another in organizing systems or leading teams.

The external label of the job may be identical, yet the internal experience can be very different.

Consider two people working in the same organization. One might spend most of their time designing strategies and solving complex problems. The other might focus on mentoring colleagues or facilitating collaboration between groups. Both roles contribute to the same organization, but they draw on different strengths.

Work tends to feel more meaningful when it draws regularly on the activities that naturally capture a person's attention.

Someone who enjoys explaining ideas may feel energized when teaching or presenting. A person fascinated by systems may feel engaged when analyzing structures or improving processes. Another who values creativity may feel most alive while designing new projects or developing original concepts.

Energy patterns often reveal these differences.

Certain tasks create a sense of focus and engagement that makes time pass quickly. Others require constant effort to maintain attention. By observing these patterns across days or weeks, individuals can begin to see which kinds of work align with their natural tendencies.

Alignment does not always require changing careers.

Sometimes small adjustments within an existing role can make a significant difference. Taking on projects that emphasize preferred skills, collaborating with colleagues whose strengths complement one's own, or shifting responsibilities slightly can gradually reshape how work is experienced.

These changes may seem modest, but over time they can transform the rhythm of everyday effort.

Work begins to feel less like constant obligation and more like a space where personal abilities can be expressed.

Reflecting on work alignment begins with simple questions.

Which parts of your work consistently generate energy and engagement? Which tasks tend to drain attention or create persistent resistance? Where do your natural interests appear within your current responsibilities?

Exploring these questions can reveal how closely your work reflects your natural patterns and where small adjustments might bring the two closer together.

18.2 Relationship Alignment

While work shapes how people spend much of their time, relationships shape how they experience themselves.

Human beings are deeply influenced by the social environments around them. Conversations, expectations, and shared values subtly guide how individuals express their interests, opinions, and aspirations. In this sense, relationships act as mirrors. They reflect back signals about what is acceptable, admirable, or discouraged.

Supportive relationships often create space for honest expression.

In such environments, individuals feel comfortable exploring ideas, asking questions, and sharing interests that may still be developing. Curiosity is met with engagement rather than dismissal. Differences in perspective are treated as opportunities for discussion rather than as threats.

These relationships provide psychological safety.

When people feel safe to express themselves, they are more likely to notice and follow their internal signals. Interests can evolve naturally, and values can be examined without constant pressure to conform.

Other social environments function differently.

Some relationships emphasize stability and predictability to such a degree that deviation feels risky. Expectations become fixed, and individuals may feel pressure to maintain roles that once made sense but no longer fully reflect who they are becoming.

In these situations, authenticity becomes more difficult.

A person might hesitate to express new interests or changing values if they fear misunderstanding or criticism. Over time, this hesitation can cause internal signals to become quieter. Curiosity is suppressed, and personal direction becomes harder to recognize.

The influence of relationships therefore extends beyond companionship.

They shape how individuals perceive their possibilities. In supportive environments, new ideas feel worth exploring. In restrictive environments, the same ideas may feel impractical or risky.

Consider how different conversations affect your thinking.

Some discussions leave you energized, thinking more deeply about ideas that matter to you. Others may subtly discourage exploration, reinforcing familiar paths even when they no longer feel meaningful.

These differences reveal how relationships can either amplify or suppress internal signals.

People often thrive when surrounded by individuals who respect their curiosity and evolving direction. Such relationships do not necessarily remove challenges or disagreements, but they maintain an atmosphere of openness and mutual respect.

Reflecting on relationship alignment therefore involves a simple observation:

Which relationships encourage you to think freely and express your interests? Which environments make it easier to follow your curiosity?

The answers to these questions often reveal how the social world around you shapes your sense of direction.

And over time, relationships can either strengthen alignment with one's internal signals or quietly weaken it.

18.3 Environmental Alignment

The environments in which people live and work quietly influence how they think, feel, and act.

Physical surroundings shape concentration and mood in ways that are often underestimated. Some people find their attention sharpens in quiet spaces where interruptions are rare. Others think more clearly in lively environments where conversation and movement stimulate ideas. Even simple elements light, noise levels, access to nature, or the layout of a workspace can influence how easily a person focuses or how creatively they think.

These effects may seem small in the moment, but over time they accumulate.

A workspace filled with constant interruptions can slowly drain attention. A crowded schedule in a chaotic environment may make thoughtful work difficult. By contrast, an environment designed for focus one that allows time for deep thinking and reduces unnecessary distractions can make complex tasks feel far more manageable.

The influence of environment extends beyond physical surroundings.

Cities, workplaces, and communities each carry their own rhythms and expectations. Some environments encourage exploration, experimentation, and intellectual exchange. Others emphasize routine, efficiency, or stability. Neither orientation is inherently better, but each one affects how individuals experience their daily lives.

Consider how different environments affect your energy.

A person drawn to creative work may feel energized in communities where new ideas circulate freely. Someone who values careful analysis may thrive in quieter settings where sustained concentration is possible. In each case, the environment interacts with the individual's natural tendencies.

Certain environments therefore amplify strengths.

When the surrounding context supports how a person naturally works and thinks, effort feels more sustainable. Creativity emerges more easily, collaboration becomes productive, and motivation remains steady.

In environments that conflict with a person's tendencies, the opposite often occurs. Energy drains more quickly, concentration becomes harder to maintain, and even familiar tasks require greater effort.

Designing an aligned life therefore involves paying attention to the environments that shape daily experience.

Sometimes alignment requires major changes, such as relocating to a different city or shifting into a different workplace culture. More often, however, small adjustments can make a meaningful difference reorganizing a workspace, finding communities that share similar interests, or structuring environments that support focused work.

These changes gradually create conditions where attention and creativity can operate more naturally.

One useful starting point is simple observation.

Where do you tend to feel most comfortable thinking and working? In which environments does your energy increase rather than decline?

The answers to these questions often reveal where your natural tendencies are most supported and where your environment may already be helping you do your best work.

18.4 Time Structure Alignment

Time is one of the most revealing indicators of what truly shapes a life.

People often describe their values in abstract terms curiosity, creativity, relationships, learning, contribution. Yet the structure of daily time frequently tells a clearer story. The activities that consistently receive time gradually become the activities that define identity.

What occupies the hours of a day slowly becomes the structure of a life.

This does not mean every hour can perfectly reflect personal priorities. Work obligations, responsibilities, and practical constraints influence how time is distributed. But even within these constraints, patterns emerge.

Some individuals devote most of their available time to immediate tasks and external demands. Others carve out regular space for learning, reflection, or creative work. Some prioritize relationships through frequent conversations and shared experiences, while others focus more heavily on solitary pursuits.

Over weeks and years, these patterns accumulate.

Routines shape habits, and habits shape identity. A person who spends consistent time exploring ideas gradually becomes more knowledgeable and intellectually curious. Someone who regularly creates writing, designing, building slowly develops creative skill. A person who invests time in relationships builds deeper connections.

In this sense, time structure quietly reinforces direction.

When daily routines align with personal values, life begins to feel more coherent. The activities that matter are not merely imagined goals but lived experiences. Interests receive enough time to develop, and priorities move from intention into practice.

Misalignment often appears when time is dominated by activities that do not reflect what a person considers meaningful.

For example, someone may value learning but rarely allocate time for reading or study. Another may care deeply about relationships yet find their schedule consistently prevents meaningful connection. In these situations, the gap between intention and routine can create a sense of quiet dissatisfaction.

Adjusting time structures does not require dramatic change.

Often small shifts are enough to begin. Setting aside a regular hour for reading, dedicating focused time to creative work, protecting moments for conversation or reflection these simple adjustments gradually reshape how time is experienced.

Over time, such routines become stable patterns.

What begins as a small decision about how to spend an hour eventually becomes part of a larger rhythm of life. Skills grow, relationships deepen, and values become visible through action rather than intention.

In this way, time structure becomes a practical expression of alignment.

The question is not only what a person hopes to value, but how those values appear in the structure of everyday life.

And often, small adjustments in daily routines repeated consistently can gradually shape a life that reflects those values more clearly.

Reflection Questions

1. What patterns appear in my attention?
2. Which activities increase my energy?
3. When did I last feel deeply engaged?

Chapter 19

Authenticity and Resistance

As people begin aligning their lives with their internal signals attention, energy, curiosity, and values an unexpected challenge often appears.

Resistance.

This resistance does not always come from within. More often, it emerges from the surrounding social world. Friends, family members, colleagues, and communities carry expectations about how a life should unfold. When someone begins adjusting their path in ways that differ from those expectations, the change can create friction.

This friction does not necessarily mean the direction is wrong.

In many cases, it reflects a simple reality: personal alignment often develops faster than social understanding. Others may still see the individual through the lens of earlier roles or past decisions. When those roles begin to shift, the change can create uncertainty not only for the person making the transition, but also for the people around them.

Living authentically therefore involves more than discovering internal direction.

It also involves learning how to navigate the social pressures, misunderstandings, and expectations that often accompany meaningful change.

19.1 Social Friction

Human relationships depend, in part, on predictability.

Over time, people come to expect certain patterns in one another. A friend is known for a particular role, a colleague for a certain skill, a family member for a specific set of priorities. These expectations help social environments function smoothly. They allow others to anticipate behavior and build a stable understanding of who someone is.

But these expectations can also create tension when change occurs.

When a person begins adjusting their life in ways that reflect deeper alignment with their internal signals, the shift can surprise those around them. A colleague who once seemed fully committed to a particular career may begin exploring a different path. A friend who previously followed familiar routines may develop new interests or priorities.

To the person experiencing the change, the shift may feel gradual and thoughtful.

They have likely spent months or even years noticing patterns of energy, curiosity, and dissatisfaction. They have reflected on what feels meaningful and what does not. The decision to move in a new direction may therefore feel like a natural step.

But to others, the change can appear sudden.

Without access to the internal signals that led to the decision, observers may interpret the shift through their own expectations. Confusion, concern, or skepticism may arise. Questions may be asked not out of hostility, but out of uncertainty about what the change represents.

Unconventional choices often intensify this reaction.

When someone steps away from widely respected paths or chooses a direction that differs from common definitions of success, the decision may challenge shared assumptions about what a responsible or successful life should look like.

This challenge can create what might be called social friction.

Conversations become more complicated. Explanations are requested. Sometimes subtle pressure appears, encouraging the person to return to a more familiar path.

Yet social friction is often a natural response to change.

Communities develop expectations over time, and when those expectations shift, a period of adjustment usually follows. The tension does not necessarily reflect hostility or rejection. Often it simply reflects the time required for others to understand a new direction.

Recognizing this dynamic can make such moments easier to navigate.

Not every expression of doubt or confusion signals that a decision is misguided. Sometimes it simply reflects the difference between internal understanding and external perception.

And in many cases, social friction is less a warning that something is wrong than a sign that genuine change is taking place.

19.2 Approval vs Alignment Trade-Off

Human beings are naturally responsive to approval.

From early childhood, social feedback helps people understand what behaviors are encouraged and what actions are discouraged. Praise, recognition, and acceptance provide reassurance that one's choices are respected within a community. Because of this, approval carries emotional comfort. It signals belonging.

In many situations, this social guidance is useful.

Encouragement can reinforce positive habits, strengthen cooperation, and help individuals develop skills within supportive environments. Yet as people grow older and begin shaping their own direction, approval and alignment do not always point in the same direction.

Alignment requires a different kind of honesty.

It involves paying attention to internal signals curiosity, energy, values, and recurring interests and allowing those signals to influence decisions. Sometimes these signals guide a person toward paths that are unfamiliar or unexpected to others.

When this happens, a quiet tension can appear.

A choice that feels internally coherent may not immediately receive external validation. Friends may question the practicality of a decision. Family members may worry about stability. Colleagues may struggle to understand why someone would step away from a respected role or opportunity.

In such moments, individuals may feel pulled between two forms of reassurance.

Approval offers comfort through acceptance. Alignment offers coherence through authenticity.

Maintaining approval may require adjusting one's choices to match shared expectations. The individual continues along familiar paths that others understand and support. This approach often preserves social harmony, but it can gradually distance a person from their own internal signals.

Choosing alignment, on the other hand, may require accepting a period of uncertainty.

Certain expectations may no longer fit. Roles that once brought recognition may feel less meaningful. In some cases, individuals may need to release the desire for immediate validation from others in order to follow directions that feel internally consistent.

This does not mean rejecting relationships or disregarding feedback.

Social perspectives can still offer valuable insight. But alignment asks a person to weigh external approval against internal coherence, recognizing that the two may not always coincide.

Over time, individuals who consistently choose alignment often discover that authenticity creates its own form of stability. Decisions begin to reflect genuine interests and values, and the life that emerges feels more integrated.

Reflecting on this trade-off can be helpful.

In which areas of your life do approval and alignment support one another?

And where might they quietly conflict?

19.3 Emotional Resilience

When people begin making choices that reflect their internal direction, they sometimes encounter criticism, doubt, or misunderstanding from others.

These reactions can trigger powerful emotional responses. Even individuals who feel confident about their decisions may experience moments of uncertainty when their choices are questioned. A skeptical comment from a colleague, concern from a family member, or subtle disapproval from peers can create the feeling that something may be wrong.

This reaction is deeply human.

Because social belonging has historically been essential for survival, criticism often activates a strong psychological response. The mind quickly searches for reassurance, asking whether the decision should be reconsidered or whether the direction being pursued is truly justified.

In some situations, this reflection can be useful. Thoughtful feedback sometimes reveals blind spots or practical concerns that deserve attention.

But not all criticism carries the same weight.

Some reactions simply reflect the perspective of the observer rather than the validity of the decision. Others arise from unfamiliarity with the path being taken. When a choice challenges established expectations, doubt from others may reflect uncertainty rather than genuine insight.

Emotional resilience helps individuals navigate these situations without becoming overwhelmed by them.

Resilience does not mean ignoring all criticism or becoming indifferent to the opinions of others. Instead, it involves developing enough internal stability to examine feedback calmly rather than reacting impulsively.

When a resilient person hears criticism, they can pause and consider the source.

Is this feedback based on experience and thoughtful concern? Or does it reflect discomfort with change?

This pause allows reflection to occur before self-doubt takes over.

Resilience also grows gradually through experience.

Each time a person makes a decision aligned with their internal signals and observes the outcome, confidence develops. Even when mistakes occur, the process of learning from those experiences strengthens the ability to trust one's judgment.

Over time, individuals begin to recognize that external opinions fluctuate.

Some people will support a decision, others will question it, and still others may remain indifferent. If every opinion carried equal weight, it would be nearly impossible to maintain a consistent direction.

Maintaining perspective therefore becomes an important skill.

Instead of reacting strongly to every reaction, resilient individuals evaluate feedback carefully while remaining grounded in their own observations and experiences.

This balance allows people to remain open to learning without becoming controlled by external judgment.

In this way, emotional resilience functions as a stabilizing force.

It allows individuals to remain steady when faced with criticism, uncertainty, or misunderstanding, continuing to move forward even when external pressure becomes strong.

19.4 Staying Grounded in Direction

Periods of resistance often create moments of doubt.

When others question a decision or react with uncertainty, it is easy for attention to shift away from the signals that originally guided the choice. The mind begins to replay external opinions, wondering whether those voices might be correct.

In such moments, remaining grounded requires returning to the internal signals that first revealed the direction.

Earlier in this book we explored how patterns of attention, energy, curiosity, and emotional response often indicate where alignment exists. These signals rarely disappear simply because others misunderstand them. What often changes is the level of confidence with which a person trusts them.

Reflection helps restore that confidence.

Revisiting the experiences that led to a decision can clarify why the path felt meaningful in the first place. A person may remember the sense of engagement that appeared during certain projects, the curiosity that repeatedly returned to a particular subject, or the quiet dissatisfaction that existed before the change.

These reflections reconnect the individual with their internal reference point.

Supportive relationships also play an important role in maintaining direction. Not everyone will understand a new path, but some people will recognize the sincerity behind it. Conversations with individuals who respect personal exploration can provide encouragement during uncertain periods.

Such relationships act as stabilizing influences.

They remind a person that growth often requires patience and that temporary uncertainty does not invalidate a meaningful direction.

Over time, consistency itself becomes a source of confidence.

As individuals continue working, learning, and experimenting along their chosen path, results begin to accumulate. Skills develop. Insights deepen. The direction that once appeared uncertain gradually becomes more coherent through experience.

Others may also begin to see the pattern.

What initially seemed unconventional may later appear intentional as the person's engagement and progress become visible.

Staying grounded therefore does not require constant certainty.

It requires ongoing attention to the signals that revealed direction and the willingness to continue acting in alignment with them. Reflection, supportive relationships, and consistent effort gradually reinforce this commitment.

In this way, alignment is not maintained through a single moment of confidence.

It is sustained through steady awareness and continued dedication to the direction that feels internally true.

Chapter 20

The Evolving Self

Throughout this book we have explored a central idea: beneath the noise of expectations, comparisons, and external pressure, individuals carry signals that reveal something about who they are and where they may be going.

These signals appear through attention, energy, emotions, recurring interests, and patterns that unfold across experience. By learning to observe them, people can begin to recognize the directions in which their lives naturally tend to move.

Yet one final insight remains important.

Direction is not a fixed destination.

Even when individuals begin living in closer alignment with their internal signals, life continues to change. Interests deepen or fade. Values evolve. Circumstances shift. What once felt central may later become less important, while new questions gradually emerge.

Recognizing this reality helps prevent a common misunderstanding.

Alignment is not about discovering a final identity that remains permanent. It is about developing the capacity to remain attentive as identity continues to unfold.

20.1 No Final Identity Exists

Many people spend years searching for a stable answer to a simple question: *Who am I?*

The question often carries an implicit expectation. Once the answer is found, it will remain consistent. A person will discover their true role, profession, or defining characteristic, and that identity will provide a reliable foundation for the rest of life.

This expectation appears in many forms.

Someone may hope to discover their "true calling." Another may search for the perfect profession that fully captures their abilities and interests. Others attempt to define themselves through a single label writer, engineer, teacher, entrepreneur believing that once the correct label is found, the uncertainty surrounding identity will disappear.

For a time, these definitions can feel reassuring.

A clear identity provides structure. It offers a way to explain one's choices and communicate them to others. When people know how to describe themselves, they often feel a greater sense of stability in the world around them.

Yet life rarely remains still long enough for any identity to remain permanent.

Experiences accumulate. New ideas appear. Skills develop that once seemed distant or unfamiliar. Interests that once felt central may gradually give way to different curiosities. Over time, these changes reshape how individuals understand themselves.

Consider how many people's interests evolve across different stages of life.

A person who once defined themselves primarily through achievement may later discover deeper satisfaction in mentoring others. Someone who spent years pursuing stability may gradually feel drawn toward exploration or creativity. Another may shift from learning new skills to sharing knowledge with others.

None of these transitions invalidate earlier identities.

Instead, they reveal how identity develops through experience. The person who becomes a mentor often draws on years of learning that came before. The individual who pursues creativity later in life may be building upon earlier periods of discipline or expertise.

Problems arise when identity becomes too rigid.

When people believe they must remain consistent with a single definition of themselves, they may resist changes that could lead to growth. A person who has invested years in a particular role may feel reluctant to explore new interests because doing so would challenge their established identity.

In such cases, the identity becomes a constraint rather than a guide.

A more flexible understanding of identity allows for adaptation.

Instead of asking, "What single definition describes me forever?" individuals can ask a different question: "How am I evolving through my experiences?"

This shift changes the nature of identity itself.

Rather than a fixed label, identity becomes a pattern that develops across time. It reflects the ongoing interaction between curiosity, experience, and learning.

Viewed this way, identity is not something that must be discovered once and preserved permanently.

It is something that continues to develop as life unfolds.

20.2 Meaning Changes Across Life

Just as identity evolves, the sources of meaning that shape a person's life also change over time.

At different stages of life, different questions become important. In earlier years, meaning often appears through exploration. People experiment with interests, develop skills, and test possibilities. Curiosity drives them toward new experiences, and much of life feels like an open landscape of potential directions.

During this period, meaning may be closely tied to discovery.

Learning something new, mastering a skill, or pursuing an opportunity can feel deeply satisfying. Progress is often measured through growth new abilities, new environments, new perspectives.

As experience accumulates, however, priorities often begin to shift.

Responsibilities increase. Relationships deepen. Work and community become more central parts of life. Meaning may gradually move from exploration toward contribution. Instead of asking, "What can I learn?" individuals may begin asking, "What can I build?" or "How can I help others grow?"

For some people, another shift appears later.

After years spent pursuing goals or fulfilling responsibilities, reflection becomes more important. Individuals may begin reconsidering the broader story of their life what experiences have taught them, what values remain most meaningful, and how they wish to spend the years ahead.

These transitions are not universal in the same way for everyone, but some pattern of evolution is common.

Priorities rarely remain identical throughout a lifetime.

Interests that once seemed unimportant may return unexpectedly. A fascination from childhood may resurface after years of dormancy. Values that once appeared secondary may gradually become central as life experience reveals their significance.

For example, someone who spent many years focused on career advancement may later rediscover the importance of creativity or intellectual curiosity. Another person who once valued independence above all else may gradually find deeper meaning in collaboration and community.

Such changes can sometimes feel unsettling.

People may worry that shifting priorities suggest inconsistency or uncertainty. Yet these changes often reflect something more constructive: the natural development of understanding.

Experience reveals dimensions of life that were previously invisible.

What seemed important at one stage was often appropriate for that moment. As circumstances and perspectives expand, the meaning that guides decisions expands as well.

Seen in this way, changing meaning does not represent instability.

It represents growth.

20.3 Staying Attentive to Signals

If identity and meaning continue to evolve, then the ability to notice internal signals becomes a lifelong skill.

Throughout this book we have explored several of these signals patterns of attention, fluctuations in energy, emotional responses, recurring interests, and the feedback that emerges through action. These signals do not disappear once a person feels more aligned with their direction. Instead, they continue to provide information as life unfolds.

Attention still reveals what captures curiosity.

Certain questions return again and again in the mind. Particular problems feel worth exploring, while others quickly fade from interest. By observing these patterns over time, individuals can notice when their curiosity begins shifting toward new areas.

Energy provides another signal.

Some activities create a sense of engagement that makes effort feel worthwhile. Others gradually drain motivation even when they appear impressive from the outside. These responses often change as experience deepens. Work that once felt challenging and stimulating may eventually feel routine, while a new area of interest may begin generating fresh excitement.

Emotions also carry information.

Moments of satisfaction, frustration, fascination, or unease often reveal how experiences interact with personal values. A feeling of excitement during a conversation may signal an emerging interest. A sense of resistance toward a long-standing responsibility may indicate that priorities are evolving.

Remaining attentive to these signals allows individuals to adapt naturally as life changes.

For example, someone who once spent years developing technical expertise may later notice a growing interest in teaching others what they have learned. Another person may realize that their curiosity is shifting toward broader questions about systems, communities, or ideas.

These changes do not require immediate decisions.

They simply invite observation. Over time, new patterns become visible. Interests that once appeared briefly may grow stronger, while others gradually fade. This process reveals how personal direction continues to develop through experience.

Curiosity about one's own development becomes an important companion in this process.

Instead of assuming that identity should remain stable, individuals can remain interested in how their patterns evolve. What captures attention now? Which activities generate energy? Which environments encourage reflection or creativity?

These questions help maintain awareness as circumstances change.

Self-awareness, in this sense, is not a single discovery but an ongoing practice.

By continuing to observe internal signals attention, energy, emotions, and patterns individuals remain connected to the evolving process through which their identity and direction continue to unfold.

20.4 Living as an Unfolding Process

As this book reaches its conclusion, a quiet realization becomes clear.

Understanding oneself is not a task that is completed once and then set aside. It is an ongoing process one that continues as long as a person remains attentive to their experiences. Each stage of life introduces new environments, new relationships, and new questions. These experiences gradually reshape how individuals understand themselves and the world around them.

Because of this, self-knowledge is never final.

The signals explored throughout this book attention, energy, curiosity, emotional responses, and recurring patterns do not lead to a single definitive answer about who a person is. Instead, they provide guidance within an evolving process. They help individuals notice how their interests develop, how their values deepen, and how their direction slowly becomes clearer through experience.

Curiosity plays an important role in this unfolding.

When people remain curious about their own development, they allow themselves to adapt rather than resist change. New ideas can be explored without the pressure to immediately redefine identity. Unexpected interests can be observed with patience rather than dismissed as distractions.

This openness allows growth to continue naturally.

Direction, in this sense, rarely appears all at once. It emerges gradually through interaction with the world. Each experience adds a small piece of understanding. A project reveals a new ability. A conversation introduces a new question. A challenge clarifies what truly matters.

Over time, these moments accumulate into patterns.

Looking back, individuals often realize that their direction was not determined by a single decision. It developed through many small adjustments choices influenced by curiosity, engagement, and reflection.

Accepting this unfolding process can also bring a certain freedom.

If life is understood as a fixed destination, uncertainty feels threatening. Every decision appears final, and every mistake seems costly. But when life is viewed as an evolving process, uncertainty becomes part of learning. Changes in interest or direction no longer appear as failures but as natural developments within a longer journey.

This perspective invites patience.

It allows individuals to move forward without demanding perfect certainty. Instead of seeking a final definition of identity, they remain attentive to the signals that appear beneath the noise of expectations and comparisons.

Those signals continue throughout life.

They appear in moments of curiosity, in activities that generate energy, in ideas that return repeatedly to the mind, and in experiences that feel quietly meaningful. By observing these signals with care, individuals remain connected to the evolving process through which their lives continue to take shape.

And so the invitation at the end of this book is simple.

Continue paying attention.

Notice what captures your curiosity. Observe where your energy rises or falls. Reflect on the patterns that appear across your experiences. Allow these signals to guide your next steps.

Life does not arrive as a finished identity.

It unfolds.

Closing Reflection

By the time you reach this final page, you may notice something subtle.

The questions that brought you to this book may no longer feel quite the same.

Perhaps you began with a sense of uncertainty about direction. Maybe there was a quiet feeling that something in your life did not fully fit, even if nothing was obviously wrong. You may have wondered whether you were missing something others seemed to possess clarity, purpose, or confidence about where their lives were going.

But one of the ideas explored throughout this book is that many people are not lost in the way they often assume.

More often, they are surrounded by noise.

Expectations about what a successful life should look like. Comparisons with the visible achievements of others. Cultural scripts about careers, status, and identity. The steady pressure to move quickly, produce results, and present certainty.

In such an environment, it becomes difficult to hear anything quieter.

Yet beneath that noise, signals continue to exist.

They appear in the activities that capture your attention without effort. In the problems that repeatedly draw your curiosity. In the moments when your energy rises and engagement deepens. In the emotions that quietly indicate when something feels meaningful or misaligned.

These signals are not dramatic.

They rarely arrive as sudden revelations. More often they appear as patterns small tendencies that repeat across time. A question that keeps returning. An interest that refuses to disappear. A sense of vitality during certain kinds of work or conversation.

For a long time, it is easy to overlook them.

But throughout this book, you have explored how those signals can be observed.

You have seen how patterns of attention reveal what the mind naturally gravitates toward. How energy fluctuations reveal where engagement appears most naturally. How emotions provide information about values and meaning. How experimentation transforms uncertainty into learning.

These observations create a shift.

Instead of searching for direction in external expectations, you begin to notice direction emerging from within your own experience.

The signals were not absent.

They were simply difficult to hear beneath the noise.

Once these signals become visible, something else becomes possible.

You can begin building from them.

Direction does not need to appear all at once. It can emerge gradually through action. Small experiments reveal preferences. Adjustments bring daily life closer to personal patterns. Work, relationships, environments, and routines slowly begin to reflect what feels internally coherent.

In this way, a life becomes something that is designed rather than discovered.

Not through a single decision, but through many small adjustments guided by observation and experience.

And even then, the process continues.

Identity evolves. Interests shift. New signals appear as life unfolds. The work of self-understanding therefore never truly ends but it also does not need to.

It becomes a practice.

A quiet form of attention to what captures your curiosity, where your energy rises, and what continues to feel meaningful.

The world will always contain noise.

Expectations will continue to exist. Comparisons will remain visible. External definitions of success will continue to circulate through culture and conversation.

But beneath that noise, something quieter remains available.

Your signals.

If there is one idea to carry forward from this book, it is not a specific answer about who you must become.

It is a simple orientation:

Pay attention.

Notice what consistently draws your curiosity. Observe where your energy appears and where it fades. Reflect on the patterns that repeat across your experiences. Allow those signals to guide your next small step.

Direction will continue to emerge through that process.

And as it does, life gradually becomes less about finding certainty and more about participating in an unfolding process of learning, adjustment, and discovery.

The signal is still there.

You only need to keep listening.

The purpose of this book was never to give you a fixed answer.

Instead, it offered a way of listening.

Signals will continue to appear throughout your life— through curiosity, energy, questions, and experience.

The task is not to eliminate uncertainty.

The task is to remain attentive to the signal beneath the noise.

Printed at Repro India Ltd.